Shop Drawings
for
Craftsman Furniture

SHOP DRAWINGS
for
CRAFTSMAN FURNITURE

27 Stickley Designs for Every Room in the Home

Measured and drawn by
ROBERT W. LANG

CAMBIUM PRESS
Bethel

Shop Drawings For Craftsman Furniture
27 Stickley Designs for Every Room in the Home

ISBN 1-892836-12-2
First printing: October 2001
Printed in Canada
Published by
    Cambium Press
    PO Box 909
    57 Stony Hill Road
    Bethel, CT 06801

Library of Congress Cataloging-in-Publication Data

Lang, Robert W. 1953-
    Shop drawings for Craftsman furniture: 27 Stickley designs for every room in the home /measured and drawn by Robert W. Lang.
    p. cm.
    ISBN 1-892836-12-2 (sc.)
    1. Furniture--Drawings. 2. Measured drawings. 3. Arts and crafts movement. I. Title.

    TT196.L35 2001
    684.1'04--dc21

2001043505

CONTENTS

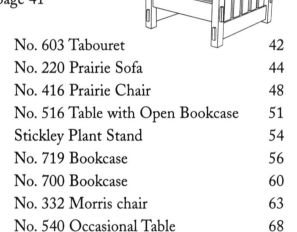

LIVING ROOM
page 41

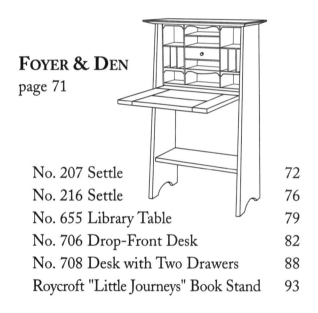

FOYER & DEN
page 71

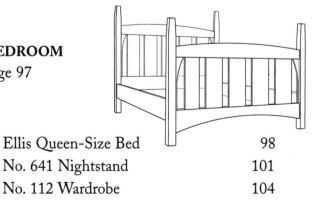

BEDROOM
page 97

DINING ROOM
page 115

Everyone knows the relief to brainworkers and to professional men that is found in this kind of work. It not only affords a wholesome change of occupation but brings into play a different set of faculties and so proves both restful and stimulating. A professional or business man who can find relief from his regular work in some such pursuit which he takes up as recreation, does better work in his own vocation because he is a healthier and better balanced man and his interest in his home grows more vivid and personal with every article of furniture that he makes with his own hand and according to his own ideas.

Gustav Stickley
Cabinet Work For Home Workers
Craftsman Homes pp.169-170

INTRODUCTION

It has been my good fortune to have spent nearly all of my adult life earning my living by working with wood. The idea to produce this book actually came to me quite some time ago, but it was always one of those projects on the "someday" list. Like most woodworkers, it takes me a while to get around to the big ones.

My first introduction to Craftsman-style furniture was in the late 1970s, and my appreciation and fascination with this style has only grown over the years. At that time I was still in the eager apprentice "soak up as much information as I possibly can" phase of my career, and some of my favorite sources were books of drawings of furniture, particularly Ejner Handberg's books on Shaker furniture and Gustave Ecke's book on Chinese furniture. The drawings in those books taught me as much or more about styles, design, and techniques than any of the other sources available to me. I kept expecting that someday someone would produce a book of drawings for Craftsman furniture.

Years passed, the book I wanted to see never appeared, and somewhere along the line I realized that I should go ahead and do it myself. I began by scaling the illustrations in reproduction catalogs, then producing working drawings by hand from that. In the process I read all that I could find about how these pieces were constructed, and took every available opportunity to observe and study actual pieces.

This is pretty much the process that was used to produce these drawings, although it has been greatly simplified thanks to the personal computer and AutoCAD software. I scan as many photographs and drawings of original pieces as I can find into AutoCAD, and adjust their size to full scale. Then it becomes a matter of making a mechanical drawing from a perspective image. Details are zoomed in and measured, and then compared to known dimensions from pieces I have measured, similar pieces, or published information. Combined with my experience in the industry, and research on this type of furniture, a relatively accurate shop drawing is then produced.

These drawings are very close to the originals, but they are not perfect—there are places where I have had to make educated guesses as to the exact size of one part or another. Usually my guesses are very close, and many of the pieces in this book that were originally drawn from photographs were later measured, confirming the accuracy of the process. In some ways, I think this lack of perfection is a good thing.

The intent of this book is to give the average woodworker or devotee of Craftsman furniture the ability to produce, for his or her own pleasure, pieces of furniture that represent the style and spirit of the originals. It is not intended to be an aid to anyone attempting to fool the collector's market by passing off new work as antiques. If your intent is to commit such fraud, please look elsewhere for an accomplice. I urge everyone building furniture from these drawings to sign and date your work to avoid future confusion.

The other issue of accuracy comes from the original pieces themselves, which often vary significantly from one example to another. This, I think, is understandable, in light of several factors. First, not everyone measures furniture in the same way. An antiques dealer or catalog copy writer without training in woodworking may ignore some of "those funny little marks" between the inches, or may not hold the tape measure squarely. Some will consider the height of a dresser to be to the top surface, while others will measure to a piece of back trim.

The other reasonable source of variation is the nature of wood, and of woodworking. Solid wood expands and contracts as humidity and temperature change. If two identical pieces of furniture leave the factory, they likely won't be exactly the same size after a hundred years, particularly if one has been taken care of and one has been abused. At a recent auction I saw three examples of Roycroft "Little Journeys" stands. The tops of all three were different dimensions, varying about half an inch from the smallest to the largest. All were authentic, yet which one was the right size? None of them exactly matched the dimensions published in reference books and auction catalogs.

Furniture made in factories is generally produced in "cuttings," representing the amount the manufacturer thinks will sell over the next few months. All of the parts for that number of pieces will be milled, then stored to be assembled as the orders come in. It is common to adjust sizes and make minor changes from one cutting to another, for reasons of appearance, improving productivity or yield, or to utilize a new piece of machinery. If someone makes a mistake and produces a batch of parts that are not quite the proper size, those parts most likely will not be thrown out, they will be used. Many of these pieces were in production for several years, and during that time quite a few minor changes were made for many reasons.

The point of all this is that while I have tried to be true to the originals, the original pieces themselves don't always match previously published information about them. The answer to the question of "how accurate are these drawings" depends on all of the above factors. They are accurate enough for today's worker to build a very nice, structurally sound piece of furniture, which will be recognized as a Craftsman piece. They are true to the style, and that is not only the best we can do today, but also the best that Stickley himself ever did.

Gustav Stickley's Craftsman Furniture logo

THE STORY OF CRAFTSMAN FURNITURE

One hundred years ago society as a whole, and the design community in particular, stood at a crossroads. The world was rapidly changing as new technologies were developed. The notion of what makes a house a home was questioned then, as it should be questioned now. The places where we spend our time and the objects with which we surround ourselves have a significant influence on our comfort, peace of mind, and well-being. Craftsman design fills both the need for usefulness and the desire for beauty. It does this in a way that expresses the inherent character of the natural materials, and the character and values of the designer and maker. It is a welcome respite from designs whose purpose is to prove the wealth of the owner or to present "newness" only for the sake of following the latest trend.

Good furniture design simply makes sense; furniture should serve its purpose as well as possible, be constructed to endure, and use materials that please the eye and hand. It should bring a sense of calm and comfort to its environment, not disturb or detract from it. Any design reflects the values and personality of the designer, the maker, and the owner. Craftsman design expresses integrity and quality in a quiet, dignified manner. It does not shout, but it cannot be ignored. It serves its purpose while providing pleasure to the senses. Good design comes, as Gustav Stickley put it, "from the bottom up." It is based on solid fundamentals, expressed in a straightforward manner.

As Stickley put it: "In the beginning there was no thought of creating a new style, only a recognition of the fact that we should have in our homes something better suited to our needs and more expressive of our character as a people than imitations of the traditional styles, and a conviction that the best way to get something better was to go directly back to plain principles of construction and apply them to the making of simple, strong, comfortable furniture that would meet adequately everything that could be required of it." (*Craftsman Homes*, pp.158-159).

It is this expression of character that separates Craftsman furniture from other styles, and the values attached to that expression are the foundation of its appeal. This appeal also comes from the bottom up—it matches a desire for things that make sense, that present themselves in an honest way and use the beauty of nature without exploitation. Like the furniture itself, the values and ideals behind the furniture have a timeless appeal to the best aspects of human nature.

Though Gustav Stickley is certainly the main character, the story of American Arts & Crafts furniture also features Gustav's four brothers, particularly his younger brother, Leopold, who was to become Gustav's biggest competitor. The five brothers were independent and strong-willed men, all successful in the furniture business but unsuccessful at working with each other. Their father abandoned the family when the boys were quite young; as they came of age, the three oldest went to work at the chair factory in Brandt, Pennsylvania, owned by their uncle, Jacob Schlaeger. In 1884, with the financial backing of another uncle, Schuyler Brandt, Gustav, Albert, and Charles formed the Stickley Brothers Company, in Binghamton, New York, which sold (and after 1886, manufactured), furniture. Leopold and John George joined the growing company around 1888.

Gustav left the family business later that same year, starting a similar business named Stickley & Simonds in partnership with Elgin A. Simonds. Although this partnership lasted only a few years, it was revived in Syracuse, New York, in 1894, and lasted until 1898. During the years in between, Gustav held positions with a streetcar company in

Binghamton and later was director of manufacturing at the New York State Prison in Auburn, New York.

Gustav was successful enough to be able to afford, in the last years of the 19th century, to tour Europe and England, surveying what was happening in the Arts & Crafts Movement. He also devoted a great deal of time to experimenting with new designs. Eventually he developed his own style, which he called "Craftsman Furniture."

Leopold left the family business about a year after Gustav and worked for him both at Stickley & Simonds and at the Craftsman shops, which Gustav established in 1898. In 1891, Charles and Schuyler Brandt took control of the operation in Binghamton (renamed The Stickley and Brandt Chair Company), while Albert and John George took the Stickley Brothers' name and established their own manufacturing business, called The Stickley Brothers Company, in Grand Rapids, Michigan.

By 1900, the Stickley brothers were well settled. Gustav was in Syracuse, Albert and John George were in Grand Rapids, and Charles was in Binghamton. Their three separate companies became four in 1902 when Leopold formed the L. & J. G. Stickley Company near Syracuse, with John George as his partner.

In Syracuse, Gustav worked at developing his new designs. His furniture was first marketed by the Tobey Company of Chicago, a distributor of furniture produced by others as well as a manufacturer. Dissatisfied with this arrangement, Gustav began marketing his own work in the early 1900s. As Gustav introduced his new designs and their style became popular, his company became successful—along with those of his brothers and numerous other competitors.

Success continued until the First World War, when popular tastes began to change. *The Craftsman* magazine was launched in

October 1901, and within a few years Gustav was seeking to expand into architecture and home construction. Furniture remained the backbone of the business, but Gustav also produced linens, rugs, and metalwork, including lamps, hardware, and accessories. This continued expansion was his financial undoing. Following all of his interests, and developing enterprises devoted to each of them, Gustav created an operation that was too complex for one person to manage.

Gustav established his corporate headquarters in a large, expensive building in New York City in 1913. He kept the Craftsman Farms in New Jersey as his residence and school. Eventually he was spending much more than he was taking in and in late 1915, Gustav filed for bankruptcy. He briefly worked as a consultant, then joined in an ill-fated venture with his brothers before retiring in 1918. His final 24 years were spent living with his daughter and grandchildren. When Gustav retired, Leopold and John George continued as the L. & J.G. Stickley Company, which is still in operation although not owned by the Stickley family. Albert and Charles continued into the 1920s with their companies.

Leopold Stickley left his brother's company in 1902 to start his own operation, financed in part by a loan from Gustav. At first he made products sold under other names, but in 1904 Leopold's own line of furniture was introduced. Focused solely on one business, and aided by brother John George, who was considered to be one of the best furniture salesmen in the country, Leopold was more successful financially than Gustav. When public tastes changed around World War I, he switched from Arts & Crafts furniture to reproductions of early American furniture. Leopold himself ran the company until his death in 1957.

Gustav Stickley and his brothers literally grew up in the furniture business, manufacturing reproduction and other popular styles of chairs, as well as marketing the work of other manufacturers. By all accounts, each brother was talented and successful. However, as with their first attempt at working together, their business relationships were on-again, off-again. Their independence and strong wills helped them to achieve business success, but apparently prevented them from working together in groups of more than two.

One of Gustav's challenges was the vast number of competitors who freely adopted his designs, including those companies owned and operated by his brothers. Similar shop-marks and similar names added fuel to the fire. Gustav's catalogs emphasized how his furniture was marked, and he occasionally took the opportunity to remind the public that "some of the most persistent of these imitators bear the same name as myself" (1910 catalog, pg. 8).

Gustav Stickley was among the first to produce this style of furniture, and one of the most successful manufacturers of his day. The sheer number of other companies that copied his work attest to his design leadership. But Stickley's impact was much broader than his furniture.

For Gustav Stickley was also a leader of the Arts & Crafts Movement, seeking to promote a better way of life based on ideals from the past adapted to a changing society. While others were trying to sell furniture, Stickley was looking at the changes that were making a tremendous impact on the way people lived and worked. The last 20 years of the 19th Century saw new ways of manufacturing, communicating, and day-to-day living. Like the computer in our own time, the technological revolution at the turn of the 20th Century was lighting homes, powering factories, and speeding up the pace of everything. The telephone was becoming common and automobiles were beginning to replace horses for transportation.

Stickley questioned whether or not people should use the new technology to do the same things faster and more cheaply, or whether new technology should be used to do things differently, to improve the quality of life for all. Quality of life was important to Stickley, and he saw both the home environment and workplace as ideal places for people to establish values of honesty and integrity. He saw cheap, poorly made furniture as a threat to the values of the American home and society. He felt that if people would surround themselves with simple, pure, humble, and honest objects, those qualities would become an inherent part of their daily lives. Driven by his ideas more than by a desire for personal wealth, Stickley couldn't stop with furniture making. He became a publisher, an educator, and a designer of homes and virtually everything that went into them.

Gustav Stickley's designs, and those created by Harvey Ellis and produced by Stickley's factory, are what everyone else at the time copied and are most of what is being reproduced today by the L. & J. G. Stickley Company and other manufacturers. William Morris and John Ruskin in England had sown the seeds for the Arts & Crafts Movement. Architects in England and America, notably Charles Rennie Macintosh, Frank Lloyd Wright, and Charles and Henry Greene, were working on similar designs, derived from the same philosophical framework. But it was Gustav Stickley who popularized the style, reaching a far greater audience than anyone else.

The basic elements of Stickley's designs— simple forms, lack of ornamentation, and high quality—expressed construction that had been seen earlier in the work of the Shakers, the English Arts & Crafts designers, and to some extent the designs of Charles Eastlake. Stickley's expression of these ideals was, however, quite different in the materials he used, in his structural composition, and in the joinery elements he emphasized. His sense of proportion, and the way in which he combined simple elements, was flawless. Gustav Stickley's

designs simply "look right." They serve their purpose superbly and make a positive statement about quality without being showy or ostentatious. His designs fit the user, the home, and their purpose, expressing the philosophy behind the designs without making that philosophy more important than the specific use of the furniture.

When Gustav Stickley first began his experiments with Arts & Crafts furniture, he tried many variations before settling on the designs that went into production. These pieces were not squared-off designs, but featured curves and decorative carvings based on plant forms. He soon decided that it was better to start with a structural idea rather than with an ornamental one. That philosophy is at the core of Stickley's designs: an eloquent expression of a purely functional item, with the structural elements themselves becoming the ornamentation.

Stickley's strength as a designer was his sense of proportion. Simple furniture is not simple to design, and with decorative elements nonexistent or kept to a minimum, a successful design must make the most of those elements that do exist, must show the materials to their best advantage, and must be balanced. While the scale of many pieces appears large when viewed in isolation, the overall scale of the furniture is often on the small side, which keeps the furniture from overwhelming its environment.

At first glance, Craftsman furniture is intriguing because it is so well proportioned and makes such good use of the material. But a quick glance is never enough. It invites a closer look, to examine the exposed joints, to take a good look at the details. This furniture makes friends with its user. Chairs invite you to sit and relax, and once seated you discover interesting details you might not have noticed before. Bookcases and china cabinets provide a safe and secure place to keep things, and by their nature let you know that what is inside is rather special. Rather than

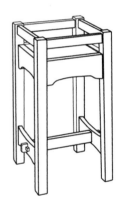

Gustav Stickley's well-proportioned designs simply "look right."

Chairs invite you to sit and relax...

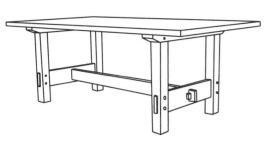

Tables provide a welcome place to gather...

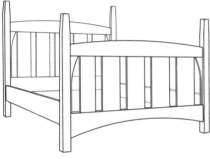

Bed by Harvey Ellis

No. 700 Bookcase by Harvey Ellis

being overpowering, this furniture invites the viewer to look closer and to use it for its intended purpose. Tables provide a welcome place for family and friends to gather, and desks give a sense of taking care of necessary business without being ostentatious. All of the elements are quite simple, but the way they are combined makes all the difference. The quality of the joinery and finish must be executed as flawlessly as possible for these designs to be successful.

After Gustav Stickley, the most influential designer of the period was Harvey Ellis, who worked for Gustav for a brief period before his untimely death in 1904. Ellis is usually described as an itinerant architect, and his addiction to alcohol caused his early death. Ellis and Stickley met in the spring of 1903, with Ellis going to work for Stickley in May or June of that year. At the beginning of the next year, Ellis was already dead, but Stickley's 1904 catalog featured many Ellis designs, notably inlaid chairs and cabinets that never went into full production, a bedroom suite (Nos. 911, 912, 913, 914), the No. 700 series of bookcases, and china cabinets, servers, and delicate small drop-front desks. The addition of arched elements, subtle curves, and purely decorative elements added a touch of lightness and grace to Stickley's previous work. These pieces are some of the best proportioned and most elegant furniture ever made.

In addition to these furniture designs, Ellis also wrote articles, designed houses, and drew illustrations for *The Craftsman* magazine. It is generally reported that Ellis was hired for his skill and training as an architect. But Ellis's talent for furniture design and the number of pieces that are attributed to him make it hard to believe that Stickley was interested in his furniture designs only as an afterthought.

Furniture production was always the largest part of Stickley's business, and faced with the ever increasing number of companies copying his work, Stickley needed new, fresh designs to stay ahead of the competition.

Many of the elements that Harvey Ellis brought to Stickley appear in pieces that didn't come into production until well after his death. It is likely that Ellis supplied the themes for these pieces, while Stickley's draftsmen worked out the details and possibly applied the themes to other pieces. Harvey Ellis strongly influenced Gustav Stickley's furniture, and many of the pieces that are considered to be the "best" examples came from him.

Lamont Warner was Gustav Stickley's head draftsman and furniture designer from 1900 to 1906. He has been credited with the design of the No. 634 five-leg cross-stretcher table (pp. 122-125). The trumpet stretchers on this table also appear on smaller tables. Again, it is not possible to say authoritatively whose idea was whose. My best guess is that much of the design work was collaborative, with Gustav supplying creative direction and general ideas for designs, while Warner, his staff, and production people all worked together to generate the details and final designs.

Leopold Stickley is also credited with all of the designs that came from his factory, and even though Leopold didn't have the demands on his time that his older brother did, it seems sensible that the L. & J. G. Stickley designs were also not the work of one man alone. According to Leopold's widow, he "roughed out" the designs (Cathers pg. 89) so others could complete them. Peter Hansen was Leopold's chief designer after 1909, but it is unknown who held the position prior to that date. Since so much of Leopold's work derived from Gustav's, the question of who designed what becomes even harder to resolve.

One of the few truly original designs to

come from L. & J.G. Stickley is the "Prairie" Sofa and Chair (Nos. 220 & 416, pgs. 44-50), which featured elements that were never included in any of Gustav's designs. The wide arms supported by corbels and paneled sides combine to form furniture pieces which, by a combination of architectural elements, become a part of their environment. Like the best Craftsman designs, these pieces blur the lines between "house" and "furniture," replacing both with "home."

Charles Limbert, a Michigan manufacturer, also was willing to experiment and innovate with designs, although some of his construction techniques have not passed the test of time. Limbert's best designs were well proportioned and included curved work, unexpected angles, and the use of empty space in cutout areas as a significant design element. Much of Limbert's work was as derivative as that of other manufacturers, but his original designs stand on their own merits.

The work of the Roycroft shop was of excellent quality but was never produced in any great quantity. Founded by Elbert Hubbard after his early retirement from a successful business career, Roycroft's primary mission was to revive the art of printing, and Hubbard's main interest was writing and publishing. Furniture production was always a sideline and while Hubbard's position in the Arts & Crafts Movement was prominent, his influence in furniture design was negligible. Much Roycroft furniture reflects English Arts & Crafts design rather than American.

The First World War and the beginning of the Roaring Twenties signaled the end of the popularity of Craftsman furniture. The desire for simplicity was replaced by a craving for glitz and glamour. Reproductions from earlier times again became popular with the public, and Art Deco design became a major influence in art and architecture. With its emphasis on form and material, Art Deco can be seen as stemming from the Arts & Crafts Movement. Straight lines

were replaced by curves, and structure and joinery were no longer emphasized. Comfort and purpose took a secondary role to overall design, and the desire to appeal to everyone was replaced by the desire to appeal to the wealthy.

Between the 1930s and the 1960s, America struggled to find furniture that it was comfortable with and could live with for more than a few years. After the Second World War many attempts were made to produce designs based on new materials such as plastics and plywood. With few exceptions, these new styles appealed only to the manufacturers, who were trying to cut costs to the minimum. Older styles were recycled in and out of fashion.

In the late 1960s people again began to question the role of technology in daily life, posing the same questions Gustav Stickley had asked many years before. Shaker furniture and the work of individual designer/craftsmen gained in influence and popularity. Like an old friend, Craftsman furniture was waiting patiently to be noticed again, enduring because of the way it was made. Its timeless quality speaks to humanity's desire for comfort and purpose in the home.

During the 1970s and 1980s interest in the Arts & Crafts Movement blossomed, not only in woodworking and furniture making but in glass, ceramics, and other crafts. By the mid-1980s furniture manufacturers recognized this revived interest and began reproducing Craftsman furniture, along with derivative designs. Collectors of antique furniture began offering higher and higher prices for original pieces. Today, the Craftsman style has a permanent place in our design vocabulary.

Five-leg cross-stretcher table attributed to Lamont Warner.

Roycroft 'Little Journeys' book stand

Prairie armchair, an original design from L. & J. G. Stickley

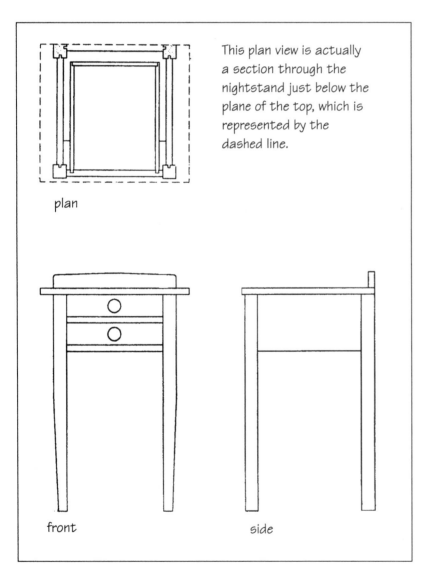

plan

This plan view is actually a section through the nightstand just below the plane of the top, which is represented by the dashed line.

front

side

INTERPRETING THE DRAWINGS

The drawings in this book have been prepared the same way that drawings are prepared in the furniture industry. In the industry, before any wood is cut, the builder will take the time to thoroughly review the drawing to be certain that his or her interpretation agrees with what is shown, and that individual techniques, preferences, and methods will produce the piece shown. Then the maker prepares a list of parts, taking into account the available materials, joinery details, and any changes that may be necessary due to these variables.

The cut lists presented in this book are what I would use in my workshop. You may work differently from me, so you should check my cut lists with care, or better yet, devise your own lists from the information given in the drawings. If you are not absolutely certain what size to make a given part, please take the time to figure it out before you cut any wood. Building a nice piece of furniture takes some time, and any time spent at the beginning of the project to understand what is to be built and how it will be built will be rewarded in the end.

Usually you will see a plan view (straight down from above), elevations (looking straight at the piece from the front or side), sections (looking straight at an imaginary slice taken through the piece), and details (either three-dimensional views, or close-up two dimensional views). Technical drawing gives a highly accurate, although somewhat unrealistic view of the three-dimensional world. Since our eyes are used to looking at three-dimensional objects, a technical drawing can be confusing, since it does not show perspective. In plans and elevations, the point of view is from a true 90-degree angle to the object and what is seen are the outlines of what is closest to the observer.

Imagine a large pane of glass placed in front of a piece of furniture, on which the image is somehow projected. Objects that are parallel to this piece of glass appear in the drawing at their true length. A line that is perpendicular to the glass would appear as a single point, and a line at any other angle, or a curve, would appear to be shortened or otherwise distorted. The three-dimensional views in this book are also prepared as mechanical representations, with parallel lines remaining parallel rather than converging as they would in real life. Because there is no foreshortening, these sometimes appear to be distorted.

Section views show the details on the inside. Imagine a hamburger, a stack (from the bottom up) of bottom bun, lettuce, tomato, meat, cheese, onion, pickle, mustard, catsup, and top bun. If you look at the sandwich directly from above, all you will see is the top bun. You know that it is round, and you can measure its diameter, but you can't tell how thick it is, or what is underneath. If you look at it directly from the front or side, you will see the edges of the bun, the meat, and perhaps a little bit of cheese or lettuce sticking out. You can measure the height and the width, but you still don't learn what is inside and you can't see that the bun is round—the edges could represent a rectangular slice of bread rather than a round bun. The two drawings together give you a good idea of the shape and size, but you still can't tell what is inside. Is there a big slice of onion, or is it chopped in tiny pieces? Did they forget the pickle, or is it above or below the meat? If you slice the burger and then look at the edge, you will get a good look at what is inside. This is the principle behind a section view, and all of the views together help you to know how the hamburger is built. If you are having trouble visualizing what a piece of furniture is really like, try looking at all the views. Something that doesn't make sense in one view usually will be shown clearly in another.

Some conventions and terms will help you interpret the drawings. Dashed lines usually represent something that is behind, or hidden by, what is in the drawing. If we are looking at the leg of a dresser where a cross rail joins it, and we see some dashed lines going into the leg from the rail, then we know that part of the rail is tenoned into a mortise in the leg. If a solid line continues out the other side of the leg, then we know that the mortise goes completely through the leg and what we are seeing is the end of the tenon on the rail.

In section views our imaginary pane of glass goes through the middle of the object, "cutting" the parts that it intersects and giving you a clear view of the parts beyond. In section views some areas will be filled in (hatched). This means that the filled part lies on the plane of the imaginary glass. In these drawings arcs or splines (squiggly lines) represent solid wood, and patterns that are more regular represent plywood, although it remains the maker's option as to what material to use. Glass is represented by its own pattern. In a section view a dashed line represents something that is in front of the cutting plane. Many of the plan views in this book are sections, or views with the top removed, with the outline of the top indicated by a dashed line.

Dimensions are indicated by extension lines and dimension lines, both of which are noticeably thinner than the lines of the actual parts of the furniture. Extension lines approach, but do not quite touch, the point on the drawing that the dimensions refer to. Dimension lines have arrowheads that either point to the extension line, or in some cases point directly to an object. Dimension lines are kept off to the edges of the drawing so that they don't interfere with the actual drawing, with extension lines connecting them to the object. Occasionally there may be confusion about where an extension line is actually pointing, but if you lay a straight edge on the extension line you will be able to see where it leads.

One of the challenges of doing drawings in

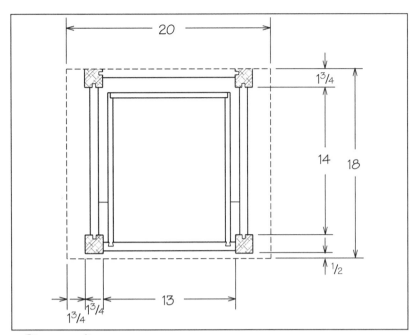

Dimenson lines and extension lines. The squiggly lines on the legs indicate they are made of solid wood.

ing cluttered and to ensure that the maker understands the drawing. It also ensures that if there is an error in the drawing or dimensions, the maker will be able to catch it and compensate for it. If the dimensions don't seem to add up, study the drawing and carefully add and subtract the sizes of the parts. Check and double check before you go cutting up your material.

The dimensions in the drawings don't necessarily reflect the total sizes of the parts. Dimensions are shown from finished surface to finished surface. Where there are openings for doors and drawers, for example, the dimensions shown are for the size of the opening. On frame-and-panel parts, the dimensions shown are for the exposed areas. The maker needs to decide how deep to make the grooves for the panels and tongues, how much of a gap to leave around doors and drawers, how much to add for tenons. This depends on many factors: personal preference, species of wood, time of year, or type of climate. You may not have access to a planer, so you decide to use the wood you have that is $25/32$" thick instead of $3/4$". There is nothing wrong with that, but if you have six rails in between seven drawers and each rail is $1/32$" oversize, you will have to compensate for the extra $3/16$" somewhere. You may not like dealing with 32nds so you decide to fudge things a little. Again, there is nothing inherently wrong in doing this, but you need to take it into account before cutting anything.

this format is to provide enough dimensions to build a piece without covering most of the page with dimension lines, arrows, and numbers. Generally, a dimension for a part is given in only one view of a drawing, hopefully in the view where it makes the most sense. The width and depth of a desktop, for example, will be located in the plan view, and the thickness of the top will be in a section view or an elevation. If it seems that a needed dimension is missing, try looking for the same object in a different view.

There will be times when it's necessary to do a little math. If there are a number of parts making up an overall dimension and the overall dimension is given, not all of the dimensions for the parts will be given. Take, for example, a plan view of a dresser. There is an overall width of the top, the width from the outside of one leg to the outside of the other leg, the width of the legs, and the widths of all the parts in between. If the parts are symmetrical, only one will be dimensioned. If you know the overall width of a paneled back, the width of one outer stile, and the width of the center stile, you can reasonably assume that both outer stiles will be the same width, and you can calculate the width of the panels in between. This is done both to keep the drawing from becom-

The pieces of furniture in this book are very adaptable, and examples of originals show variations not only in sizes but also in the material used for various parts. Some production runs were made using solid, v-grooved and splined, or ship-lapped backs, while in other years the same pieces were manufactured with plywood or paneled backs. Some items were shown in catalogs with paneled sides, yet the only known examples have solid or plywood sides. You may be a purist, and nothing but a hand-cut dovetailed drawer in solid maple will be acceptable. Or, you may prefer biscuit-joined plywood drawers. This book gives you a place to start, and the information you need to make your own decisions.

Preparing a cut list, deciding how to join one piece of wood to another, what order to assemble, and understanding the consequences of all these decisions are part of learning how to organize a bunch of pieces of wood into an attractive piece of furniture. Understanding and interpreting what is shown in a drawing, and translating that into a finished piece of furniture, is a major part of learning the entire process of building furniture.

The way that you measure, mill stock, and make joints will all affect the size of the parts needed to build this furniture. For details that cannot be seen in the original pieces, such as mortises that are not exposed or grooves in panels, I have used my own judgment based on my experience. You might not agree with my decisions, and for this reason many of the smallest dimensions in this book are not given, leaving the reader to decide whether panels should be set in a $^3/_8$" deep groove or a $^1/_2$" deep groove. All of the information needed to generate your own cut list is in the drawing, but each maker must be responsible for determining the finished size of all of the parts.

GUIDELINES FOR PREPARING YOUR OWN CUT LISTS

Let's use the No. 913 bureau on page 110 as an example of how to prepare a list of parts.

In this book, the following conventions are used when discussing thickness, width and length. When referring to pieces of wood, these terms reflect the direction of the grain. When referring to the piece of furniture as a whole, they refer to the piece's normal orien-

tation in space, and apply no matter what view of the drawing we are looking at. This may seem like a minor point, but adopting a standard and sticking to it avoids much confusion. When looking at the drawings, the whole piece is 50" high, 36" wide, and 20" deep, the way it appears when looking at the front elevation. By keeping these terms consistent, regardless of the view, we can generate a more accurate cut list and avoid errors and parts with the wood grain going in the wrong direction.

No. 913 Bureau

For individual parts, width is always the direction across the wood grain, and length is always the direction with the grain. The top of the dresser is $^{13}/_{16}$" thick, 20" wide, and 36" long, even though the width of the dresser is determined by the length of the top. A drawer opening is $4^3/_8$" high by $13^{25}/_{32}$" wide. The drawer front that goes into the opening is $4^3/_8$" wide (minus the desired gap around the opening) by $13^{25}/_{32}$" long. This convention, when adhered to, keeps the grain running the right way for all parts. In the example above, we know that the grain on the drawer front runs horizontally. If the dimension were stated the other way—$13^{25}/_{32}$" wide by $4^3/_8$" high—it would indicate that the grain runs up and down. The depth of a drawer is the distance from the front to the back, not from the bottom to the top. The drawers in this piece of furniture are all the same depth, but the second drawer up from the bottom is the tallest one.

I start by making a list of the major components, such as the top, the sides, the back, the front rails, and the drawers, leaving room on the paper to list the parts that make up these components. For this dresser, I will have:

One top—which may be composed of one or more pieces of solid wood or plywood. There is also a backsplash across the back of the top.

Two sides—composed of legs, stiles (frame parts that go up and down), rails (frame pieces that go horizontally), and panels.

No. 913 Bureau, which also appears at larger scale
on pages 110 to 113

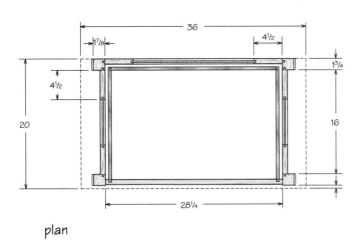

plan

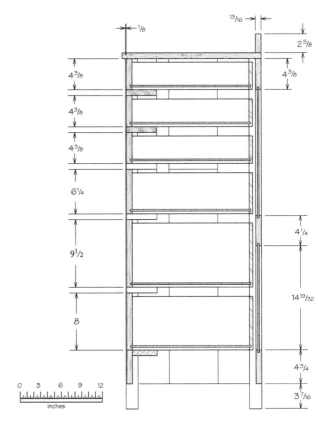

side section

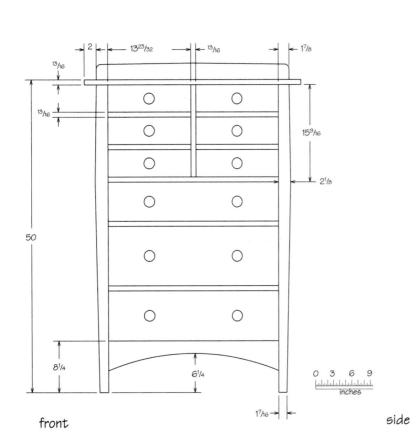

front

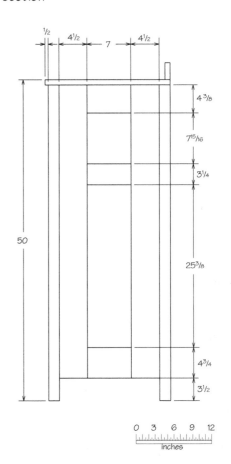

side

One back—which may be frame-and-panel construction as shown, solid-wood planks, or plywood.

Several front rails and one center stile.

Nine drawers and drawer fronts.

In addition, there are a dozen knobs or drawer pulls, and some way must be provided to slide the drawers in and out, either on purchased hardware or on guides fabricated from wood.

Looking at the drawing, I know that the finished top is $13/16$" thick, 20" wide, and 36" long. I probably don't have a piece of wood that wide, so the top may comprise two, three, or even four pieces of wood, and if gluing up for width, the individual pieces should be a little wider than necessary to allow for making the joint. My preference is to start my list with the largest pieces first, since these will have the greatest impact on the finished piece of furniture. That way, when digging through a stack of lumber, I will be looking for the widest, most attractive pieces first.

I may decide to use some lumber for the top that is already planed to $3/4$" thick. This decision won't have a tremendous impact on the appearance of the finished piece, but I must keep in mind that the $1/16$" I've just eliminated from the top thickness has to come from somewhere. I would most likely let the overall height be a little shorter, but someone else might decide to lengthen the legs. If this is done, again, somewhere in the height, the dimensions noted in the drawing will change. Making these decisions now, and noting where the changes will occur, will avoid much frustration later on.

Having determined the parts and their sizes for making the top, I move on to the other parts that appear in the front elevation. Once again, the question of thickness arises when looking at the rails between the drawers. These are stated to be $13/16$" thick, but I

might reasonably decide to use some $3/4$" thick stock. If I do, then I must recalculate the layout where these pieces meet the legs, or I will end up with a $5/16$" discrepancy.

At this point it would be helpful to take a scrap piece of wood, cut it to the length of the finished leg, and do a full-size layout. When changing the thickness of any component, it's safest to work from the middle of each joint rather than from the spaces between the parts.

By laying out full size, locating the midpoints and from them the edges, you will end up with a full-size layout to help you visualize the relationships, and you will be better able to plan your work. A calculator that can add and subtract in fractions is a tremendous help. I use a "Construction Master," which works to 64ths of an inch. Some of the other brands available will only work to 16ths of an inch, and this isn't fine enough for quality work. If you decide to ignore all of these $1/32$" differences, their feelings will get hurt and they will all get together and travel to one point of your project to accumulate against you. You won't know which point until you find yourself trying to put something together that just won't fit. It will be off by the sum of all the little discrepancies that you ignored.

The section view gives the width of the rails, and the plan view gives the distance between the front legs, which is the length of the rails less whatever is needed to make the joints between the rails and the legs. The drawings show tenons on the rails and mortises in the legs, but without exact dimensions. The builder must decide on joint details and must account for whatever effect that decision will have on the finished length of the parts.

Now that I have determined the sizes of the rails between the drawers, I can list the drawer fronts themselves, with the drawer boxes appearing as a sublist. Knowing the sizes of the openings for the drawers, either from the drawing or from calculations that include any changes, the width and length of the drawer fronts can be determined. The desired gap around the drawer front must be considered at some point, and will be based on the species and cut of wood used, atmospheric conditions both in the shop and in the furniture's future home, and the preferences of the maker.

Returning to the list of major components, the pieces for the sides can be determined by studying the drawing, listing the various parts, laying out to full size, and deciding on and noting the joinery details and how these will affect the overall sizes. The side view of the dresser tells me that the exposed portion of the stiles on the side panels is $4\frac{1}{2}$" wide; however, by looking at the section I can see that the rail fits into a groove cut into the leg, so it must be made wider to allow for the tongue. Here is yet another case where the individual maker must decide how to join the stile to the leg, and the effect that decision will have on the overall width of the stile. This same caveat applies to the sizing of the rails, and the panels that make up the sides of the case. The drawings show what the outcome should look like, but the reader needs to determine for himself the final sizes of the component parts.

The back is not shown in elevation anywhere, but the sizes for all of the parts can be determined from the top section and side section views. The method of making the back should be determined, the overall size established, and then the sizes of the component parts figured.

After the list of all the parts is completed and double-checked with the drawing, then the process of fabricating parts and building the furniture can begin. It is beyond the scope of this book to cover all of the techniques and options for milling joints and assembling furniture. If you are new to woodworking, the Bibliography lists many resources for this information. If there is a woodworking club in your area, attend some meetings and get to know other woodworkers.

Many community colleges and high schools offer woodworking classes. These can be a tremendous resource for meeting other woodworkers, learning from the instructors, and for access to machinery and tools. The chapters that follow discuss some of the various techniques used in the Stickley workshops, with tips for either duplicating these techniques or using alternative techniques that were not available in the early 1900s. The furniture presented in this book is generally straightforward and simple. However, there usually is no place to cover up less than perfect work. The results you achieve will depend on your experience and the time and care you devote to your project. If you don't feel confident in your abilities or your personal safety, take some time to develop your basic skills before attempting a large project.

Building any of the pieces of furniture in this book can be an opportunity to learn much about the process of woodworking, as well as about excellence in design. It is also an opportunity to learn new things about yourself and the way you think and work.

MATERIALS & HARDWARE

SOLID WOOD

The most common wood used in Craftsman furniture was quartersawn white oak, although many pieces were also originally made from mahogany and a few were made of bird's eye or curly maple. The current line of reproductions being manufactured by L. & J.G. Stickley is also available in cherry, a wood that works well for this style of furniture. Virtually any fine cabinet wood would work, as one of the key elements of these designs is the role that the grain, texture, and figure of the wood is allowed to play. The individual's taste, budget, and sense of history will all be involved in the decision of which species to use and whether or not to build entirely from solid wood or a combination of solids and veneers.

I would avoid the softer woods, such as poplar or pine, which won't hold up well, and plain-sawn red oak, which, despite its wide use, is too coarse and unstable for fine furniture. This furniture deserves not only your best effort but also the nicest materials that you can obtain.

Quartersawn white oak is not commonly available, and it's not inexpensive. This method of sawing does not give the yield that comes from plain-sawing and therefore the price is higher. You may have to do a bit of digging to find it, depending on where you live. There are a few sources that ship nationally, but the cost of shipping will increase the cost significantly.

If you haven't worked much with solid wood, it would be worthwhile to read *Understanding Wood*, by R. Bruce Hoadley. Solid wood differs from many materials, particularly other materials used for precise work. One of the biggest challenges in

woodworking is doing precision work with a material that keeps changing in size in response to changes in the humidity of its environment. This movement can be reduced to some extent by the finish applied, but it cannot be eliminated. Attempts to ignore wood movement or to restrain it will inevitably end in failure. It is a powerful force of nature and it can be understood and accommodated, but not stopped.

Seasonal wood movement varies from species to species, and the selection of species used in a piece of furniture will affect many decisions that must be made during the building process. Woods that are considered suitable for fine furniture generally are reasonably stable once dried.

The biggest mistakes that I have seen people make, and which I myself have made, involve rushing into the building process without allowing the wood enough time to reach equilibrium with the temperature and humidity of the shop. Likewise it is folly to perform the work in an environment that is quite different from the environment where the finished piece will be placed.

Kiln-dried wood is often thought to be insurance against wood movement, but once the wood comes out of the kiln it will take on moisture from the atmosphere until it reaches equilibrium with its environment. Air-dried wood and kiln-dried wood stored in the same conditions will eventually come to the same moisture content.

A good moisture meter is not cheap, but it will let you know the state your wood is in when you receive it, let you know when it has been conditioned to your shop environment, and help you spot any "wild" boards that are either unusually wet or dry. Without a meter you are left to guesswork. Where I live the summers are humid and the winters are cold and dry, so there is quite a swing in relative humidity as the seasons turn. Your area may be quite different, but you should be aware of

what is likely to happen and be prepared to work with the wood, not against it.

When you work with wood that has not been conditioned to the shop environment, the newly cut surfaces will have different moisture contents and are likely to warp or twist as the wood seeks equilibrium. Even if the wood does not warp it will change noticeably in size in a short period of time. Joints cut from damp wood recently brought into a dry shop will shrink overnight and not fit the next day. The opposite effect will occur with dry wood brought into a damp shop. I have learned to be patient, to wait a few weeks, and to compare the moisture content of lumber brought into the shop with similar pieces that have been there for a while.

The biggest problems with wood movement will occur in the widest and thickest pieces, particularly solid-wood tops and case sides, and wide doors and tall drawer fronts. Woodworkers over the centuries have learned how to allow for wood movement and the original makers of Craftsman furniture mostly followed these techniques.

Here are the main points about working with solid wood:

—Plan the gaps around doors and drawers according to the season, your shop environment, and the environment where the finished piece will be placed.

—Fasten tabletops or other wide pieces of solid wood in a way that allows for the expansion and contraction that will occur.

—Finish all surfaces the same way, with the same number of coats of the same finish.

—Don't force the wood into place with clamps. If you straighten out a crooked piece of wood by bending, eventually it will "remember" that it prefers being crooked, and will someday return to that state, even it has to crack to do so.

—Make joints that fit snugly. No glue will successfully fill gaps in joints for very long. The piece may hold together long enough to get it out of your shop, but eventually it will fail.

The other important factor in working with solid wood is to buy it from a reliable supplier, preferably from stock that has been on hand for a while. If your dealer has accepted a load of wood fresh from the kiln and passed it directly along to you without waiting for it to settle down, you could experience problems with wood movement.

If wood bends as you cut it, or splits as you near the end of a rip, it has been "stressed" or "case hardened" during drying. This means the surfaces of the lumber were dried too quickly, shrinking the cells so much that the moisture on the inside cannot readily escape. Be especially careful during all cutting operations in case this happens, and if it does, be prepared for more problems later on. If your supplier won't replace the wood (go ahead and ask, but don't hold your breath), cut parts enough over-size so that you can re-straighten them if need be, and let them adjust to the shop environment for a few weeks between rough and finish milling.

VENEERS & PLYWOOD

Veneers and plywoods were used in original Craftsman pieces, and there is no reason not to use them in reproductions. For paneled backs, dust panels, drawer bottoms, and the side panels of some cases, plywood is clearly a good choice. It is less susceptible to seasonal changes than solid wood, it is stable in thin sheets, and it can be less expensive than solid wood.

Furniture-quality plywood can be difficult to find, and your local lumberyard or big-box home center probably won't have what you are looking for. Companies that specialize in supplying woodworking hobbyists charge a premium for this type of material. The best source will be a company that supplies pro-

fessional cabinet shops and architectural millwork companies. They will have access to a wide variety of cores, thicknesses, and species, though they may not like to make small sales to individuals. A local cabinet shop may be willing to order some for you, but remember that their time is money, so don't waste it, and offer some compensation for their efforts.

Particleboard and medium density fiberboard (MDF) are probably the better choice for veneer core materials than regular plywood, which is known as veneer core in the industry. The quality of particleboard and fiberboard cores has improved greatly over the last 20 years, while the quality of veneer core material has steadily gone downhill. In particular it has become thinner than its nominal size as a way for producers to save material costs. Don't believe stories about "metric" sizes— $3/4$" plywood barely measures $11/16$" for the same reasons that 1-pound coffee cans now weigh in at 13 ounces. The "new convenient size" saves money for the producer.

The cores are not only thinner, they are not of the same quality material that formerly was used. Poplar has taken the place of birch. Thickness will be inconsistent throughout the sheet and the coarse grain of the core will likely telegraph through the veneer during finishing, creating a rough surface on what was once a smooth panel. Some plywood is also laminated before being thoroughly dry, which makes it likely to warp. Imported Lauan plywood cores are especially prone to this kind of stress, and will often bend while being cut. If you do use veneer core plywood, be sure to mill any joints in a way that will ensure a consistent thickness in the joint.

Particleboard and MDF have been the subject of much engineering work and most of the problems that used to be associated with these materials are no longer present. MDF will have a smoother, more consistent surface than particleboard, but it does tend to split when fasteners are used on the edges. These materials will warp if treated differently on opposite sides, so if you do your own veneering be sure to veneer and finish both sides. Veneering or otherwise sealing any edges that are exposed to the air is also a good idea to prevent the panels from warping.

For thin panels, such as ¼" thick drawer bottoms or back panels, veneer core is probably the better choice because it is stronger than particleboard. For drawer bottoms in bedroom cases, aromatic cedar plywood is a nice touch, although it can be hard to find.

HARDWARE

Reproductions of original hand-hammered copper hardware are available, but tend to be expensive because of the handwork required. There are a lot of "Mission style" pulls and strap hinges on the market that aren't as costly, but they're also not as nice. An alternative to metal pulls is wooden knobs, either turned or sawn square with a pyramid shape. There are a variety of sources for wood knobs, or you can make them yourself.

Original pieces were shown in catalogs and manufactured both ways, probably to offer an alternative in pricing, because hand-hammered copper hardware was as expensive a century ago as it is now. Both looks are authentic, so which to choose is a matter of your budget and personal taste.

Hinges on the original pieces were considerably heavier than anything available today. Butt hinges on originals tend to have longer leaves than today's hinges, and the barrels are of a larger diameter. Doors on the originals generally are still swinging nicely after nearly one hundred years, so the choice of hardware should go to the nicest available.

Drawers on original Craftsman pieces were usually guided by a center-mounted dovetail-shaped rail on the bottom of the drawer. The reproductions currently produced by L.

& J.G. Stickley use both this center guide and rails in the sides of the drawers. Modern metal slides can be used, although they will make the purist cringe. Accuride makes the most reliable slides; their model #3832 is a good choice for a full-extension slide. Most of the European hardware manufacturers, such as Grass, Mepla, and Blum, offer bottom-mounted ball-bearing glides that are entirely hidden when the drawer is open, making these more acceptable (and more expensive) than the Accuride. Any of these mechanical slides can be used in the pieces in this book, just be sure before starting construction that you understand how they mount and how their use affects the size of doors and drawer boxes.

Mirrors on bedroom cases swing on a fitting designed especially for that purpose, and the hardware used on the original Craftsman pieces was the same as used on most other furniture manufactured at the time. These fittings are available from mail-order suppliers of woodworking materials and reproduction hardware.

WOODWORKING TECHNIQUES

This is a book about furniture construction, not a basic woodworking text. Different methods will be discussed, in the context of this style of furniture and in specific pieces, but the reader without much experience would benefit greatly from practice in basic joinery before attempting a major piece of furniture. There is no substitute for practical experience. The Bibliography (page 143) contains a list of books that I have found helpful over the years. In addition, in many areas it's possible to gain experience through woodworking classes or clubs. Woodworking is not something to approach lightly, given the inherent danger of the tools involved. Therefore, never attempt a technique that doesn't feel safe, and practice different techniques on scrap wood before embarking on the real project. Seek the advice of experienced woodworkers as needed, and if you get the feeling that something you are about to do is risky, it probably is. Stop and examine ways to work safely before proceeding.

A large part of the preparation for building furniture is consideration of which technique to use to make each joint. There really isn't a "right" or "wrong" way, there is simply a variety of choices based on a maker's tools, skills, and experience. There are many different ways to accomplish any task, and one of the pleasures of learning to work with wood is the discovery of the ways that work best in any given situation.

The simplicity of Craftsman furniture designs could lead one to believe that it is simple to make. This simplicity, however, carries with it a need to truly master basic skills, and to apply them with care and forethought. There are no moldings to cover gaps, and with so much exposed joinery, there is no place to cover up errors. An exposed, keyed mortise-and-tenon joint makes a statement about its maker. Like a sports team that wins the championship due to mastery of the basics, a successful piece of Craftsman furniture will be made by someone who has the patience to master the fine points of joinery and the confidence to let it show.

The choices I make about the techniques to use can vary widely depending on whether I am making furniture to sell, for my own use, or simply for the experience and the opportunity to learn something new. Sometimes the choice is to use machinery, and sometimes it is to do the work by hand. Usually it is some combination of the two. I am always amused by those who claim some sort of moral superiority for using a hand technique over a machine. Each method has advantages and disadvantages, and either can be appropriate in some circumstances and not in others. The choice of which to use is simply personal preference based on the job, the tools, and the available time. Knowledge of several different methods gives the builder more options.

Sometimes the "right" choice is a hand plane or scraper, and sometimes it is a plunge router. It is definitely worthwhile to have the ability to hand-plane and scrape a solid-wood top to a flat, level, and smooth surface, and it is a pleasurable, gratifying experience. It is also a lot of work and it takes time. If that time is not available, and if my old-time woodworker ego doesn't need to be stroked, I would choose to use a wide-belt thicknessing sander. In another situation I might choose a quiet afternoon, a physical workout, and a pile of shavings on the floor.

My preferences are simply that, and I encourage readers to explore all the available options and adopt the ones that are most suitable. There are as many ways to make a mortise and tenon as there are ways to skin a cat. The trick is to find a few that you are comfortable with, that succeed most of the time, and that make your woodworking more enjoyable. We learn and develop our skills by trying things we haven't tried before; we won't learn anything new and we won't grow when we decide that there is only one right way to accomplish any given task.

SOLID-WOOD TOPS

Solid-wood tops are included in nearly every piece featured in this book, except, of course, chairs. The original makers were faced with the same decision that today's woodworker must make, namely how to make a wide top from narrow boards. Except for the work of L. & J. G. Stickley, which used splines, most tops were made by simply butt-joining the pieces. The main advantage of using splines, or the modern alternative of biscuits, is not a matter of adding strength, since an edge-grain to edge-grain glue joint is very strong to begin with, but a method of keeping the pieces aligned during glue-up. As long as the edges are square and smooth, an edge-grain to edge-grain butt joint is extremely strong and stable. Battens clamped above and below the pieces being joined, in addition to the clamps holding the parts together, will keep the pieces nice and flat. It is well worth the extra effort at this point, because removing a lot of material after glue-up isn't much fun however you choose to do it.

Much has been written about orienting the boards to be glued to prevent cupping. One popular theory is that alternating the planks so that the bark side is up or down on every other piece will prevent the top from warping. The important issues in making a solid-wood top, however, are appearance and longevity—you want the top to stay together forever. A solid-wood top on a nice piece of furniture should appear to be a single board, and if stable, seasoned stock is used, with finish applied equally on all surfaces, and care is taken in design and construction, it doesn't matter a bit which way the boards face. I like to start a furniture project by gluing up the top. I select the wood from the widest, longest, most attractive boards and arrange them so that they look as much like a single piece of wood as possible.

match parts for a top is by [...] arts as possible either from [...] from boards that were cut [...] equence. By doing this task [...] ailable lumber can be examined and compared. My approach is to go through the stack of lumber, picking out likely candidates for the top, and setting them aside after sketching the rough sizes on the surface with chalk or a lumber crayon. Long pieces will be cut to a rough length, and after all have been milled to a consistent thickness, the pieces can be arranged in different ways until an acceptable appearance is found. Once this decision has been made, I draw a triangle on the surface to maintain the desired orientation.

I prefer to joint the edges just before glue-up, and even though I am confident in the squarenesss of the jointer's fence and table, I alternate the face of every other edge against the fence. This ensures that even if the edges are slightly out of square, the angles will be complementary and the resulting joint will be flat across the faces. It is a lot easier to make a perfect top from perfect pieces, and my preference is to have the edges as straight as possible. Another bit of nonsense passed off as good practice is to plane a slight bow in the edges so that they must be forced together by the clamps. In my experience, wood placed under stress during glue-up will eventually "relax" and crack at the joint. If the stock is at equilibrium with the shop environment, and it has been milled carefully, the parts used in the top will not need great pressure to be brought together and they can be expected to stay together.

I usually glue up a top an inch or so wider than what I need, and several inches longer. I alternate clamps above and below the surface so that they are pulling as close to the center of each board as possible. I check to make sure that I haven't put any kind of bow or twist into the top, and I'm also careful about how much glue I use.

As a young apprentice being instructed in gluing, I jumped into the conversation about thirty seconds too soon and said, "the glue should squeeze out so I know I've used enough, right?" The journeyman instructing me looked me right in the eye and replied, "The glue should almost squeeze out so you don't make a mess you'll have to clean up later on." At the time I thought he was nuts and way too picky, but I have over the years become just as nuts and just as picky. I don't like to waste glue any more than I like to waste any other material, and cleaning up a lot of glue squeeze-out is not only messy, it can get glue in places you don't want it and won't be able to see until it ruins your first attempt at putting on a finish. Judging the amount of glue to use isn't that difficult, just one more skill that will come from practice.

If I do have any squeeze-out, I make sure to remove it before the glue dries hard. I use an old scraper or the back of a wide chisel to get it off, not a wet rag, which often just thins the glue out and spreads it all around. Leaving beads of glue on the surface will slow down the drying process, and weaken the joint at that point. The other big problem with leaving squeeze-out on the surface is that you eventually must remove it. A thoroughly dry bead of glue is incredibly hard. Trying to take it off with a hand plane is hard on the edge, trying to sand it off is hard on whatever type of sander is used, and it is easy to tip a belt sander balanced on a bead of glue and gouge the wood.

Once the glue has dried, it's time to smooth the wood and cut it to finished size. With the top the right size, the glue joints will need to be evened up and the entire top will need to be made smooth enough for finishing. I think that finding a wide belt sander large enough to send the completed top through is the best alternative. Many shops will let you use theirs for a reasonable price. A decent hand plane in capable hands is probably the next most efficient alternative.

Table iron

Table buttons

Taper jig
consists of a
plywood sled with
screwed-down
blocks to hold
the workpiece in
place.

Once again, the belt sander is an alternative, but I don't think it offers any advantage either in efficiency or quality over the plane and scraper. It takes about as much skill to guide a belt sander to good results as it does to guide a plane, and the chances of doing some damage with the belt sander are higher. Factor in the noise and dust of the belt sander versus the good workout from the plane and scraper, and make your choice.

With the top complete except for the final finish sanding or scraping, how is it held down to the rest of the furniture piece? Most of the original examples featured in this book were attached with "table irons." These are figure-eight-shaped pieces of metal that are screwed down to a rail on one end and up to the top on the other. They are available from mail-order and internet woodworking hardware suppliers. These allow for the top to be pulled down flush, and also will shift as the wood in the top expands and contracts. The side that attaches to the rail needs to go in a counterbored hole that partially intersects the inner edge of the rail. The best way to make this counterbore is with a Forstner bit, because it leaves a flat bottom and also will cut neatly through the edge of the rail. Avoid the temptation to be cheap by using a spade bit. The cut through the edge of the rail will be ragged, but more importantly, the pilot will leave a hole too large for the screw to grab. After making the counterbore with the Forstner bit, drill a separate pilot hole for the screw into the rail. Be extremely careful when drilling the pilot hole that goes up into the top. If the top is around $3/4$" thick, there will not be many threads in that screw that will be able to grab. Use a tapered bit and be careful to match the depth of the hole to the length of the screw.

The common alternative to table irons are shop-made table "buttons." These small blocks of wood have a rabbet on one end that slips into a groove on the inside of the rail. They work well, but require more effort to make. The most important thing to remember when attaching the top is that it will expand and contract, and this movement cannot be restrained or prevented. If you screw it down, be sure that there is a way for the screws to move along with the wood.

LEGS

Many of the legs in Craftsman furniture are too thick to be made from a single piece of wood. The original makers had various ways of dealing with the situation. The problem is not only one of stability of construction, but also of appearance, particularly when working with quartersawn oak. Oak cut in this way is absolutely beautiful on the face, but can be scruffy on the edges. Gustav Stickley laminated legs, gluing two or more pieces together to achieve the desired thickness. The solid faces were oriented to the front of the piece of furniture, and the sides of the legs were often veneered. Nearly all of the original pieces that I have seen have exhibited some form of cracking along the lines of the laminations, usually near the floor. Since quartersawn wood moves more in thickness than width, this cracking is not unexpected.

In other woods, such as mahogany or bird's eye maple, the difference in appearance between the face and edge grain is not as great and laminated legs could look good without veneering. Leopold Stickley made legs from four pieces of wood joined at each corner with a mitered rabbet. This allows thinner stock, and provides face grain on all four sides. These joints could be simply mitered, but the rabbets keeps the miters from sliding during gluing. A similar joint can be made with a lock miter shaper cutter or router bit. Mitered joints with biscuits are another alternative, and if solid stock is available, the only reason not to use a solid piece, provided that the wood is thoroughly dry and at equilibrium with its environment, would be the difference in appearance between the quartersawn face and the edges.

Craftsman-style legs often are tapered on one or more edges. The most reliable way I have found to taper legs is to cut them slightly oversize, either on the bandsaw or with a jig on the table saw, then remove the saw marks with the jointer or a hand plane. For cutting on the table saw, I use a sled of plywood a few inches wider and longer than the leg as the base for a jig. One edge of this is run through the blade, and the fence is kept in the position used for this cut. The cuts are laid out directly on the leg, and these marks are then placed on the freshly cut edge. Blocks of scrap are then screwed down to the plywood sled to hold the leg from behind and on the side that is not being cut. With the saw blade raised to cut the full thickness of the leg, the jig is pulled back behind the blade, the leg placed upon it, held down with a toggle clamp if necessary, and the sled is pushed through the blade with the other edge pushed against the fence as in a normal rip cut. This jig can be put together quickly, and works better than the adjustable tapering jigs that are available commercially.

FRAMES & PANELS

Much of the furniture in this book features frame-and-panel construction for doors, case sides, or as an alternative to a plank-constructed back. These are straightforward tongue-and-groove constructions, without any decorative molding. There are some variations: In some pieces the legs take the place of the stiles, and in others, the stiles have a tongue on the outer edges that fits into a stopped groove in the leg. At the corners, a long tenon (sometimes reinforced with a dowel), fits into a mortise deeper than the groove provided for the panel. Many of the original panels were veneered, which was probably a better choice than using solid wood for these relatively thin, wide panels. Most of the drawings show $\frac{1}{2}$" thick plywood with a tongue worked around the edges for the panels. These could easily be replaced with a piece of $\frac{1}{4}$" plywood, the way paneled backs are shown in the drawings.

The thinner plywood will have a greater tendency to warp, and the quality and thickness of the core can cause problems in appearance and require a slightly different technique for making the grooves. Most dado setups cannot mill a groove narrower than $\frac{1}{4}$" wide, and nominal $\frac{1}{4}$" thick plywood is undersized enough so that there will be a visible gap between the frame components and the panel itself. The easiest solution is to use a stackable slot-cutting setup in a router table to mill the grooves, instead of a dado head setup on the table saw. These cutters are available in increments of $\frac{1}{32}$" so a good fit can usually be achieved.

Glass doors and case sides are joined in a similar fashion to panels; however, instead of grooves, the back sides of the frame members have a rabbet for the glass with removable stops behind the glass. Generally, the corners of the stops are mitered, and the stops are held in place with small brads. This is a reasonable alternative for panels as well.

Making good panels is mainly a matter of starting with good parts and working precisely. All surfaces should be square, true, and of a consistent size. Saw marks from ripping the stock for stiles and rails should be removed before assembly. If these pieces are ripped slightly oversize, they can be sent through the thickness planer up on edge, in groups of several pieces. Ganging the pieces in this way helps keep them from tipping on their way through the planer, and will ensure that the size is consistent.

The joints can be cut in a number of ways, the important point being that the parts are held tightly against the fence and the table surface during cutting. Featherboards and other hold-downs not only increase safety, they increase accuracy by keeping the stock where it should be for cutting. Care taken at this stage will be appreciated at the next stage, when the joints must be cleaned up. It's a good idea to make practice joints on scrap wood and to save parts from a successful joint as an aid in setting up the next time.

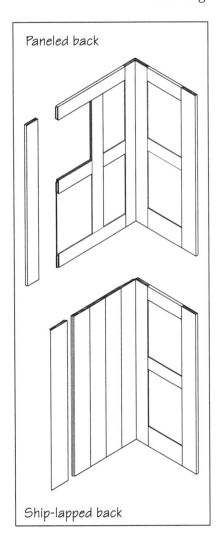

Paneled back

Ship-lapped back

In gluing up frames and panels, many workers make the stiles and rails slightly oversize so they can trim the entire panel to size after assembly. In my opinion this practice complicates the process and encourages sloppy work. For the panel to look right in the end, the joints need to be assembled tight and square, and any trimming should leave parts that are parallel to each other at the same exact width. If I am capable of working that precisely, then I don't need to leave extra to be trimmed for the sake of trimming. The exception is paneled doors, which I make to the size of the opening, and then trim to achieve the desired gap around the edges.

Some pieces have a single flat panel for the side, instead of a framed panel. A number of pieces were shown both ways in catalogs, and this is always an option whenever a frame-and-panel side is shown. While these panels can be made from solid wood, it would be prudent to use a veneered panel instead, made either from a sheet of hardwood plywood, or veneered by the maker. Both sides—back and front—of the panel should be veneered to equalize the movement of moisture through the panel, and it should be finished on both sides as well.

Dust panels were occasionally used in some of the originals, but not in others. To avoid complicating the drawings in this book, they have not been included in any of the pieces. If these panels are desired, it is a simple matter to construct a four-sided frame with the front rail as shown in the drawings, and a piece of ¼" thick plywood trapped in a groove in all four pieces.

BACKS

The earlier pieces of Craftsman furniture usually had backs made up of individual planks, chamfered on the long edges and joined together with splines at each joint. As time went on, these were replaced in the manufacturing process with either frame-and-panel backs with thin veneer panels, or with thicker plywood backs as a single unframed panel. The drawings show different styles in different pieces, but these should not be taken as hard and fast rules. The maker will need to decide which style and method should be used.

The advantages of a single-piece ¾" or ½" thick plywood back are simplicity of construction and overall stability. There is only one piece to be cut to size, and seasonal wood movement won't be a factor. If the back is exposed, as in the case of an open or glass-door bookcase or china cabinet, the appearance won't be quite as nice as a framed panel or plank back.

Solid-wood backs require a bit of planning regarding seasonal wood movement, and a few steps in construction to accommodate this movement. An alternative to the splined back is the ship-lapped back. In either case, some space should be allowed for the wood to either expand or contract, depending on the season of construction. This will vary with the wood species, and R. Bruce Hoadley's *Understanding Wood* provides some methods for calculating this movement in various species. If using the splined back, the splines themselves should be of the same species as the wood of the planks, as there will be times when they will be exposed to view, however slightly. If the v-groove appearance of the splined back is preferred, the edges of the shiplapped pieces can just as easily be chamfered. The advantage of the shiplap is there are fewer pieces to make and fit. The disadvantage is that if any of the individual planks start to bow, they will not be held in place by the adjacent plank. The back pieces should not be glued to each other, nor to the case itself, except along the long edges at the cabinet sides. Each individual plank should be fastened top and bottom with one fastener in the center of the plank. This fastener can be either a nail, which will bend slightly as the wood moves, or a screw in an oversized hole. This keeps each plank in its relative position, but leaves it free to expand and contract in width. If the back were glued together to form one piece, as in a solid top, the total movement could force the case sides apart. Keeping the planks separate will show slight gaps between them during the driest season. These gaps will then expose either the splines or the shiplap on the neighboring piece.

MISCELLANEOUS CASE JOINTS

In several pieces the legs form a part of the frame-and-panel structure either by replacing the stiles, or by having the stiles joined to the legs. The joints for these are shown clearly in the drawings, but the reader should be aware that grooves in the legs for this purpose will have a definite stopping point near the end of the panel toward the bottom of the piece. I prefer to make these stopped grooves with a spiral cutting bit in the router table rather than with a dado head in the table saw. Either method makes an acceptable groove, but the dado head will leave a substantial ramp where the groove stops, and it will either have to be cleaned out by hand or dealt with in some other manner. It would also be wise not to carry the groove completely to the intersection of the rail, but to stop it $\frac{1}{4}$" to $\frac{1}{2}$" further up, and take a slight notch out of the corresponding rail. This will ensure that none of the groove is exposed after assembly.

In pieces where there is a single wide piece of wood between the legs, the reader is again advised to give careful consideration to using a veneered panel product rather than solid wood. Most original pieces of this form were actually veneered, and the ones that used solid wood can often be identified by the cracks that have formed over time. Solid wood can successfully be used, but the carcase must be constructed so that the movement of the solid side pieces is not restrained by another component.

Rails between doors and drawers are shown to be joined by mortise and tenon to either a vertical stile or, more often, to the front leg of the case. This is authentic construction, but the sizes shown in the drawings reflect my own preferences. An alternative to mortises and tenons, and probably a superior method to the original construction, is to put a dovetail on the ends of the rails. The dovetail will fit a corresponding socket either routed or chiseled from the back side of the leg or stile. This is the method used by the current L. & J.G. Stickley Company for their reproductions of Craftsman furniture. Once set up, milling these joints is a little faster than making the mortises and tenons and offers a mechanical advantage should any parts shrink over time.

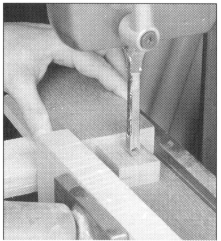

Hollow-chisel mortiser makes square corners, ideal for Craftsman furniture.

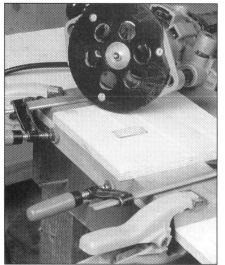

Mortising. Router bit with guide collar follows cutout in plywood template clamped to workpiece.

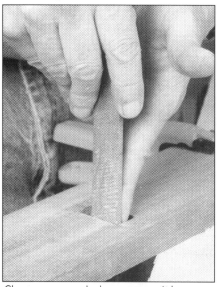

Clean up rounded corners with rasp.

MORTISE & TENON

One of the hallmarks of Craftsman furniture is the through-mortise-with-exposed-tenon joint. Often the tenon extends far enough to allow the cutting of a second mortise; inserting a wedge-shaped key locks the joint. Through mortises really aren't any more difficult to make than hidden mortise-and-tenon joints—the difference is similar to singing in the shower and singing before an audience. Any mortise-and-tenon joint must be precisely made if it is to serve its function over time, but when the joint is exposed, extra care needs to be taken, since the appearance of the joint is so important to the appearance of the entire piece. Parts that are usually hidden from view become finished surfaces, and there is a significant difference between a mortise and tenon that is ready to be glued together and one that has an acceptable finished surface.

The problem is that there is a built-in limit as to how far one can go in making these surfaces smooth before the fit of the joint becomes too loose. How much to take off to make the joint smooth depends on how the joint is cut in the first place, and there are numerous options. Many of the keyed tenons are too long to be cut with a tenoning jig on a table saw. These cuts may be made with a well-tuned band saw, and the option of cutting them by hand with either a tenon saw, or a Japanese saw should be considered. In any case, the quality of the work at this point takes precedence over speed, and it would be worthwhile to make a few practice joints to find a technique that works for you. My preference is to cut the tenon a little oversize, and

trim to fit with a shoulder plane followed by a cabinet scraper. I check the thickness and width with a dial caliper rather than trying to force the joint.

There are also numerous methods for cutting the mortises, and again, exposed joints will require a great deal of care. Whatever method is used for the actual cutting, cut in from the finished side as well as the hidden side to avoid tearing out the grain. Scoring around the layout lines with a sharp knife will help to ensure clean edges on the exposed side of the joint.

My first choice for mortising is a hollow chisel mortiser. Low-priced hollow chisel mortisers have become available in the last few years, and are a welcome addition to a shop making this sort of furniture. Dedicated mortisers will perform better than drill-press attachments, but the smaller versions are underpowered and must be used at a pace that doesn't force the work. The more expensive models not only offer more power, but also a cross-slide table, which securely holds the work and moves it back and forth in a straight line. While this machine will greatly speed the work, the quality of the cuts made are dependent on the quality of the chisels and bits used and the way they are sharpened and maintained. Even when optimally tuned, hollow chisel mortisers tend to be a little uneven, showing marks at each place the chisel is plunged in. Exposed mortises will probably need a little bit of handwork with either a chisel or a file to get nice crisp edges. I find that a plastic laminate file works well.

When using a hollow chisel mortiser,

it is important to stagger the cuts so that the bit and chisel are either completely embedded in the wood or are taking a cut with two sides in the wood. Trying to continue a cut with three sides in the wood will cause the bit to lean in the direction of least resistance, and will damage the bit and chisel.

A plunge router equipped with a fence or some other sort of guide is a good alternative for making mortises and useful for other tasks as well. For mortising, a 3HP model is preferable to a 1½HP model. The collet should be long enough to hold the bit securely. A spiral cut bit will give the best results.

If routing the mortise, I prefer to remove most of the waste by drilling, as this reduces the stress, strain, and noise produced by this operation. The router will leave rounded corners, which will have to be cleaned up by hand with a chisel. A chisel with a good flat back is essential. By starting the cut with the chisel angled and resting on the flat part of the mortise cut by the router, the working end can be swung into the corner and then brought straight by tilting the handle end toward the vertical, and then working down. Of course, the mortises can be made entirely by hand, drilling out most of the waste with a slightly smaller bit in the drill press.

The angled mortises that receive keys will need some handwork to angle the side that matches the wedge. Generally these wedge-shaped keys are cut at an angle of between 5 and 10 degrees, but the exact angle is not as important as getting a good match between the mortise and the wedge. It is easier to lay this out if the top of the mortise is made ¹⁄₁₆" to ¹⁄₈" larger than the bottom, depending on the thickness. Or the layout can be made on the wedge itself, making the top perhaps ¼" larger than the bottom, and then simply transferring the angle from the wedge to the edge of the tenon that is to receive the angled mortise.

While this joint appears sturdy, the weak point is at the end of the tenon that has the angled mortise cut into it. It is quite possible to split the wood at this point by using too much force to drive the wedge home. Make sure the pieces are well matched, and listen as the wedge gets tight. It will make a different sound when it seats. Clamp the pieces together before tapping the wedge home—use it to hold the joint tight, not to pull the joint together.

On the originals, all the edges of both the exposed tenon and the wedge are either rounded or chamfered, these cuts tapering down to the corner where the tenon comes through the side of the case. Often the wedge will have a slight notch cut about 1" down from the top to provide a surface for knocking it out of its seat.

Pegged mortises are common, and the biggest problem may be finding a

Table-saw the tenon shoulders.

With the shoulders sawn, remove the cheek waste on the bandsaw.

Chisel an angled face on the mortise for the wedge.

Tapping home the locking wedge.

Bending thin laminates around a form.

When this happens, the surface area of the two parts of the joint is reduced to nearly nothing, and the joint will come apart. Nearly every antique that I have seen with failing joints has been of dowel construction, and nearly every mortise-and-tenon joint I have seen has remained secure.

CURVED PARTS

Curved aprons, case sides, and corbels can be laid out from the drawings. Usually on long arcs, such as front aprons, the arc starts about 1/2" from where the end meets the leg; after cutting the curve the intersection between this small flat and the start of the curve is rounded slightly. It is usually easier to cut tenons or other joints before cutting the curve. Dimensions for the radius are usually given, but it is not always convenient to draw the arc with a trammel or beam compass. If you lay out parallel lines on a piece of tracing paper (1/8" apart if the scale is 1 1/2" = 1'), and comparable lines 1" apart on your workpiece, you can plot out the points of the curve. Bending a thin strip of scrap across these points (this may take three hands), will allow you to draw the curve, which can be cut with a band saw or jig saw.

dowel of the right size and species. A few woodworking suppliers carry them, or if a lathe is available they can be turned in the shop. Sorby makes a sizing tool that works well for this purpose because it can be set to size directly on the bit to be used for drilling the peg hole. Dowels can also be made by driving an octagonal blank through a succession of oversized holes drilled in a piece of 1/4" thick steel, ending up with a hole the desired size. Four or five holes drilled in 1/32" increments works: The edges of the steel will shave the wood to the proper size.

I have seen it advised to drill the hole in the tenon slightly off center from the hole in the mortise, in order to use the dowel to force the joint together. This is not a good practice, because it will either crush the wood at the edge of the hole in the tenon or make the dowel so difficult to drive that it may split. Drill the hole through the mortise first, clamp the joint tightly together, and then drill through the tenon and tap in the dowel.

Dowel construction might seem to be an alternative to mortise-and-tenon joints, but I would not recommend it. Dowels never expand and contract at the same pace as the surrounding wood, and eventually either the dowel or the hole becomes out-of-round.

Parts that are curved in plan, such as table aprons, were often cut from solid stock, one of the few areas where the original makers used a technique that won't hold up over time. This leaves weak "short grain" near the ends, which is likely to break. These parts are better made by lamination, either from solid stock, 5 or 6 pieces 1/8" to 3/16" in thickness, or from plywood. Nominal 3/8" thick "bending ply" or "wacky wood" is available from some sources. It is made from lauan or Philippine mahogany and is of inconsistent thickness, with a fairly rough surface that will need some filling and sanding before veneering. Birch plywood door skin at 1/8" thick is a better choice, but involves more work, since there will be more pieces. Make a form from particleboard in the correct radius—subtract the thickness from the outside radius given in the drawing, and continue in a straight line for a few inches beyond the end of the arc. Cut the plys about ¼" wider and longer than necessary. Apply glue evenly to each ply and clamp to the form. I prefer to use reactive polyurethane glue for this work rather than yellow glue, because it won't introduce moisture into the middle of these parts, and it dries more rigidly, reducing the tendency of the curved part to spring back toward its original straight form.

After the glue is thoroughly dry, one edge can be run over the jointer, and the curved piece can be ripped to final width. Be extremely careful when doing this. Keep the face tight to the jointer fence, and watch where your fingers are. When ripping, keep the face down on the saw table at the front edge of the blade, and again be aware of where your fingers are.

Curved rails on the backs of chairs were usually steam-bent on originals. This is a rather involved process, and most contemporary workers favor laminating these types of parts.

No matter how the curve is formed, the joints (usually tenons) will need to be worked after the curve is formed. This represents a slight challenge, but not an insurmountable one. A jig of some sort must be devised to safely carry the curved piece past the cutter used to form the tenon. Scrap plywood or particleboard cut to the shape of the outside radius can be attached to a sled that rides either on the surface of the machine table or vertically along an extended fence. The important thing is to be sure that the work is held securely, and there is no danger of it shifting while being cut.

A good alternative to a traditional tenon at this joint would be a pair of biscuits or some other form of loose tenon. The big advantage is that the part will need to be presented to the cutter only once, to form the slot, as opposed to four times if you are cutting a traditional tenon. Of course, if configuring and

building the jig for cutting takes longer than it would take to cut the joint by hand, there is no advantage to making this joint by machine.

DOORS

Doors are mainly frame-and-panel construction, quite similar to the panel construction discussed earlier. On some pieces the doors are solid slabs. With a solid door, more consideration must be given to wood movement, as solid wood will gain and lose some width over the seasons. This would be another place where a veneered panel might be better than a solid-wood slab. If made from solid wood, the wood must be well seasoned and stable, and a decision must be made regarding the size of the gaps around the perimeter of the door. My preference is for gaps that are as small as possible. I make a reasonable guess as to how far the wood might expand and contract, and add the total amount of the gaps to the widest width.

In either case it is important that the door be flat, the corners square, and the edges parallel both to each other and to the opening. Techniques for construction and trimming to final size have been covered previously under the topics of frames and panels and solid-wood tops.

The act of hanging doors is intimidating to many, but it is mainly a matter of working precisely and carefully on a small scale. In most of the original pieces the doors are hung on good-quality butt or strap hinges that are longer and heavier than those commonly used today. In these pieces, the doors still swing smoothly after 100 years of use. Don't expect good results from sloppy hardware, and give yourself plenty of time to get it right the first time.

Most of the doors on the pieces in this book are set slightly behind the edges of their openings. These details are noted in the drawings, but could be easily overlooked. Sometimes a thin strip of wood is added to

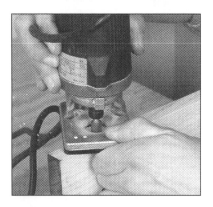

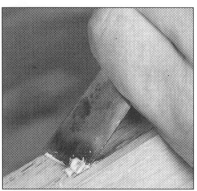

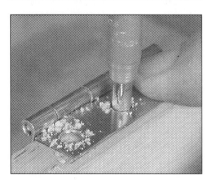

the inside of the leg or stile to carry the hinge. This piece lies in the same plane as the door, and provides some space for the hinge barrel on the outside of the door. It may be necessary to cut a small recess for the hinge barrel on the leg or stile if this piece is not present.

Once the locations for the hinges have been determined, careful layout is critical. I mark the lines with a sharp knife, and then use a laminate trimmer or the smallest router available to waste out most of the hinge mortise. The smaller router is easy to balance and control on the edge of the door, and if it is difficult to keep the base of the router flat, a piece of extra stock can be clamped flush with the edge to give the router a wider bearing surface. Guides and stops can be set to limit the router cuts to the exact size of the mortise, but my preference is to rout freehand, stopping the cuts about $1/8$" from the layout lines. I set the depth of the cutter directly from the leaf of the hinge by inverting the router, with the power cord unplugged.

The knife marks from the layout provide a place for the edge of the chisel to rest, and I use the widest chisel possible to minimize the number of cuts that must be made. If the mortise does not go entirely through the edge of the stile, the cuts on the long, narrow edge that is left must be delicately made, for it is remarkably easy to split this piece off the stile, and remarkably difficult to glue it back exactly where it belongs. The condition of the back of the chisel is as important as the condition of the edge. If the chisel back is nice and flat, it will be guided by the flat surface left by the router, pushed gently in toward the relief cuts previously made down from the layout lines.

If the mortise is carefully made, the

hinge should sit in it firmly, and the locations for the screw holes can be marked and drilled with the hinge in place. If these holes are not drilled dead center in the hole on the hinges, there will be problems. Self-centering bits (Vix bits) work well, provided that the drill is held firmly in the countersink and at a 90-degree angle to the hinge. The only drawback to the Vix bit is that it doesn't drill a tapered hole. A self-centering punch is also available, which will mark the location for the hole for drilling with a tapered bit of the appropriate size.

Setting the hinges is the time to find the screwdriver that you haven't used since you got your battery-powered drill. Finesse rather than force is essential, for the screws must be seated carefully if they are not to be damaged or stripped in their holes. If brass screws are provided with the hinges, they should not be used the first time the hinge is set because the soft brass is easy to damage. Instead, use a steel screw of the exact same size to cut the threads for the brass screw. A bit of beeswax, not soap, can be used to lubricate the screw, making it easier to turn. Soap will attract moisture from the surrounding wood to the screw location. Beeswax can be obtained from any hardware store in the form of a toilet bowl ring at a small fraction of the cost of beeswax sold specifically for lubricating screws. One toilet ring can supply your needs for life. I keep a glob from the ring in an empty 35mm film canister.

On the edge of the door opposite the hinges some means must be provided to keep the door from swinging in too far. Generally this is done by either gluing a thin strip of wood the proper distance behind the door at the top or bottom or on the long edge, or by cutting a rabbet into the edge of the stile.

Gluing in the extra strip is preferred, because it can be put off until near the end of the project and thus can be located exactly based on the actual size of the hung door. While the rabbeted stop looks a little nicer, its location must be determined at an early stage of construction, whereupon any necessary adjustments become difficult to make.

Any hardware used to keep the door closed or locked should be as carefully located and set as the hinges. If the door does not swing properly or does not look right in its opening it is possible to make some adjustments, but these are time-consuming and the results are not always successful. A veneer or paper shim can be placed behind a hinge to move it into the opening, but if much movement is required, it will show on the stile side of the hinge. Screw holes can be relocated, but the old holes must be filled as completely as possible with slivers of wood and glue. Allow the glue to dry completely or else the screw in the new hole will drift into the old hole.

DRAWERS

One hundred years from now, when your great-grandchildren are admiring the furniture you made, they should be as impressed with how nice the drawers are as your spouse will be today. Because of the many possible methods of building and hanging drawers, the details in the individual drawings have been left vague, usually indicating only the overall size of the finished drawer. In the original pieces drawers were mainly joined with half-blind dovetails at the front. The backs were dovetailed or dadoed into the sides and the bottoms were set into grooves in the sides. This is standard, quality construction and is highly recommended.

Usually the drawers on the original pieces slide on a wooden guide rail running from the front rail to the back of the case, with a matching guide block on the bottom of the drawer. In other pieces, the drawers slide directly on the bottom edges of the drawer sides, guided by blocks added to the case at the sides to prevent side-to-side movement. I prefer to hang drawers from their sides, on wood rails that ride in a shallow groove ploughed in the drawer side. The center guide method works well, but its attachment to the front rail tends to work loose over time, and it must be carefully squared front to back. Rails attached to the sides of the case should end up square to the front if the case was properly assembled, and they can be shimmed from behind if needed. Letting the bottoms of the drawer sides serve as runners will wear the parts of the case that they run on, eventually forming groves in the front rail and causing the drawer front to jam.

Maple is a good choice for drawer stock, although it is a lot more expensive than it used to be. I will often use cherry, walnut, or quartersawn oak that contains sapwood or is otherwise not attractive enough to use as a primary wood. Poplar is often used, but it is rather soft and won't wear well. It also moves more than the harder woods, as does plain-sawn oak. Bottoms are commonly made from ¼" thick plywood—birch or maple will match the drawer sides, and aromatic cedar plywood, although hard to find, will add a nice touch to bedroom furniture.

It is important to take great care in the construction of the drawers as well as in their openings. The front must be securely attached to the sides and some form of dovetail joint is preferred, because it provides a mechanical connection as well as a glue joint. This joint bears the weight of the drawer, its contents, and whatever resistance there is to movement every time it is opened or closed. It makes no difference whether you cut the drawer dovetails by hand or with a router jig. I like the Leigh jig because it allows for variable spacing of the tails and pins, making for attractive joints that can be produced relatively quickly.

Backs of drawers don't have as much force constantly applied to them, so a dado into

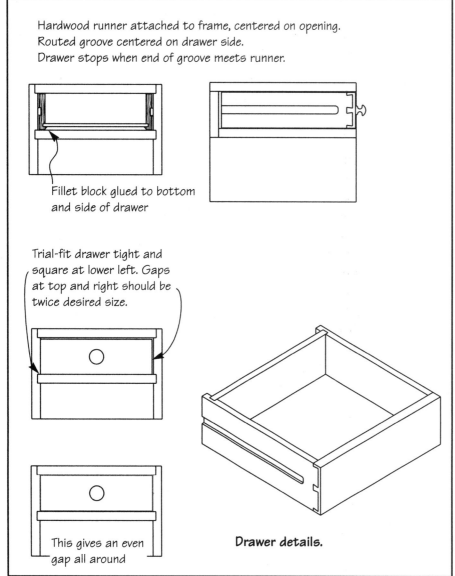

Hardwood runner attached to frame, centered on opening.
Routed groove centered on drawer side.
Drawer stops when end of groove meets runner.

Fillet block glued to bottom and side of drawer

Trial-fit drawer tight and square at lower left. Gaps at top and right should be twice desired size.

This gives an even gap all around

Drawer details.

For drawers to slide in and out effortlessly, they and their openings must be square and parallel. Even with commercial slides, this is the most important factor in how well the drawer works. There are ways to fudge and adjust after the fact, but it is much easier to fit a square drawer into a parallel opening than it is to correct the problem later on.

I like to have the drawers slide on wooden runners mounted on the inside of the case and riding in a groove in the drawer sides. These grooves need to stop behind the front edge of the drawer side so they won't show on the finished front nor interfere with the front joints. While these grooves can be made on the table saw, routing the groove keeps the bottom flat and consistent. It's simplest to leave the groove in the drawer sides rounded from the router and then round the ends of the runners to match. Centering the groove vertically on the drawer side makes the setup easy. On a typical $1/2$" thick drawer side, I make the groove $1/8$" to $3/16$" thick, and $1/2$" to $5/8$" wide.

The runners themselves need to be made from a durable, stable wood. Quartersawn walnut and cherry are ideal. If cut from thick stock, they should be given some time to reach equilibrium with the shop atmosphere before final milling.

To mount the runners vertically, I set them centered in the drawer opening and set the distance from the front with an adjustable square. Then I use the square to locate the front edge of the runner on the inside of the case. When the drawer is slid in to its opening, the end of the runner stops the drawer just inside the opening. Two or three countersunk screws attach the runner to the side of the case. This makes it easy to remove and adjust the runners.

the drawer sides works well, although many people prefer a dovetail at the back also. Bottoms need to be set in grooves with small wooden fillets or a bead of hot glue to reinforce this joint. This reinforcement not only will keep the bottom secure, it also helps to hold the drawer box itself square. If the bottom of the drawer back ends at the top of the groove for the drawer bottom, then the bottom can be slid into place after the drawer is assembled. This makes finishing the drawer box much easier. After the box is assembled and finished I put corner clamps on the front two corners to keep it square, slide the bottom in place, and glue in the fillets. The back of the bottom is then either screwed or stapled to the bottom of the drawer back.

Sizing the runners can be tricky—if they are too big the drawer will stick, but if they are too small the drawer will be sloppy. I find that making the runner $^1/_{32}$" narrower than the width of the groove is about right, and that the distance between the two runners should be between $^1/_{32}$" and $^1/_{16}$" more than the distance between the bottoms of the grooves in the drawer sides. If the drawer sticks or binds, rub colored chalk or crayon onto the runners, and slide the drawer into place. Remove the drawer and the chalk marks will show where it rubs. The high spots can then be planed or sanded down. Paraffin, paste wax, or Teflon-based spray lubricants (like Top Coat) will keep the drawer sliding smoothly.

FINISHING

Oak Craftsman furniture with its original finish is either a light or dark color, the light being close to the natural color of the wood mellowed with age. Medium Walnut Watco Oil or American Walnut Minwax stain come close to the darker color. If you are trying to closely match the original colors, a color photograph from a book or magazine will help.

A satin sheen is appropriate, whether it is achieved with oil and wax, lacquer, polyurethane, or other varnish. The finish should not be allowed to build up too thick on the oak, so that it leaves a somewhat textured, but not filled, finish.

Fuming is a good technique for coloring quartersawn white oak, but it must be remembered that ammonia can be toxic. Household ammonia is too weak to be effective but 26% ammonia can be obtained from companies that make blueprints, and while you are there please note the blurry demeanor of the employees who breathe ammonia fumes all day. When working with ammonia wear a proper respirator, not a dust mask, don't use metal containers, and never mix it with any other chemicals.

Fuming will be most successful if all the wood in the piece comes from the same log, as it is a chemical reaction between the ammonia and the tannic acid in the wood that causes the color change. The tannic content varies from tree to tree. An airtight tent is quick to put together from plastic sheeting and scrap lumber. Place the tent over the completed piece with a bowl of ammonia inside, and leave it for 12 to 48 hours. A test on some scrap from the project will show you how long it takes to achieve the desired color. Unevenness of color can be touched up with alcohol-based or oil-based aniline dyes. Water-based dyes can raise the grain, which would then require some sanding that might go through the color.

Mahogany pieces were not colored heavily, just a bit of brown to come very close to "traditional" mahogany finishes. Some that were finished quite dark now appear nearly black. The maple pieces are not common, and the only example I have seen was in curly maple with a dark brown, rather muddy looking color . The old catalogs list a "silver gray" finish on maple, which Stickley describes as being achieved by brushing on a solution of vinegar that has had rusty iron soaking in it for a few days. I haven't seen an original example of this, and I have never tried this treatment on maple, but I have successfully ebonized walnut with this same solution.

Use white vinegar and any rusty scrap metal or steel wool, which will degrade quickly in the solution. As the metal soaks it releases iron oxide into the solution, which will react with chemicals in the wood in different ways in different species. Do not let the rusty metal soak in a sealed container, because gas forms during the process and can build up to an explosion.

LIVING ROOM

No. 700 Bookcase
page 60

No. 332 Morris Chair
page 63

No. 516 Table with Open Bookcase
page 51

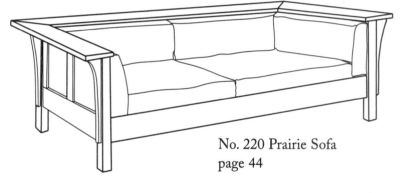

No. 220 Prairie Sofa
page 44

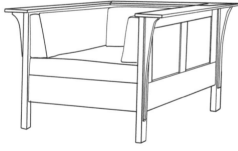

No. 416 Prairie Chair
page 48

No. 603 Tabouret
page 42

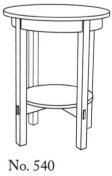

No. 540
Occasional Table
page 68

Plant Stand
page 54

No. 719 Bookcase
page 56

Gustav Stickley

NO. 603 TABOURET

18" dia. x 20" high

Because of its construction, the tabouret is a very sturdy little piece, suitable for use as an end table, TV table, or plant stand. You could also press it into service as a place to park your lap-top computer, though you might want to increase the height by a few inches.

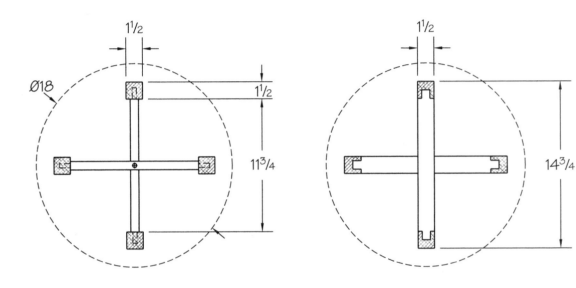

plan

front

0   3   6   9   12

inches

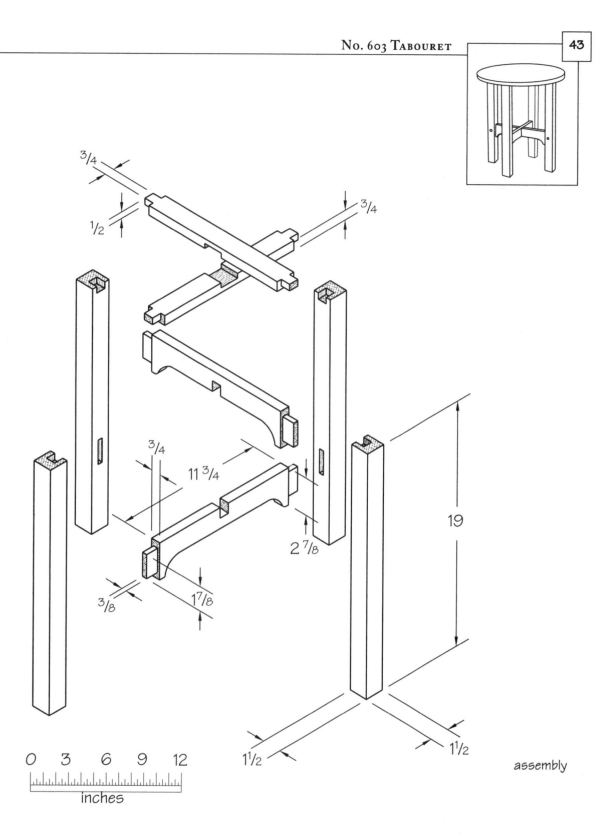

3/4

1/2

3/4

3/4

11 3/4

2 7/8

19

3/8

1 7/8

1 1/2

1 1/2

assembly

0 3 6 9 12

inches

	Gustav Stickley No. 603 Tabouret		
Qty	Part	Size	Notes
1	Top	1 x 18 dia.	
4	Legs	1½ x 1½ x 19	
2	Top Stretchers	¾ x 1½ x 13¼	half lap in middle
2	Bot. Stretchers	¾ x 2⅞ x 13¾	11¾ between tenon shoulders

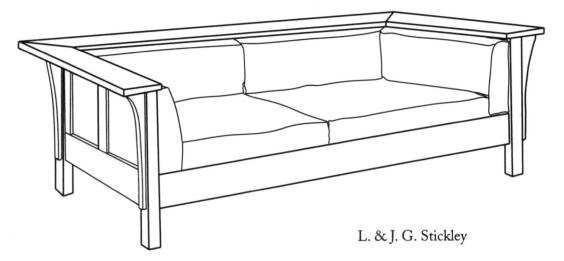

L. & J. G. Stickley

NO. 220 PRAIRIE SOFA
29" high x 84 1/2" wide x 36 3/4" deep

The Prairie settle or sofa and chair (page 48) represent a truly distinct design from Leopold Stickley. Unlike anything ever created in Gustav's workshops, this suite is a classic example of excellent Arts & Crafts design.

L. & J.G. Stickley No. 220 Praire Sofa

QTY	PART	SIZE	NOTES
4	Legs	$2^{15}/_{16}$ x $2^{15}/_{16}$ x $28^{3}/_{16}$	
2	Side Panels	$^{13}/_{16}$ x $27^{9}/_{16}$ x $21^{11}/_{16}$	$26^{1}/_{16}$ x $21^{11}/_{16}$ exposed—parts detailed below
4	Side Outer Stiles	$^{13}/_{16}$ x $3^{1}/_{8}$ x $15^{11}/_{16}$	$2^{3}/_{8}$ x $15^{3}/_{16}$ exposed
2	Side Middle Stiles	$^{13}/_{16}$ x $2^{3}/_{8}$ x $12^{15}/_{16}$	$11^{15}/_{16}$ between tongues
2	Side Top Rails	$^{13}/_{16}$ x $3^{1}/_{4}$ x $22^{5}/_{16}$	$21^{5}/_{16}$ between tongues
2	Side Bottom Rails	$^{13}/_{16}$ x $6^{1}/_{2}$ x $27^{9}/_{16}$	$26^{1}/_{16}$ between tenon shoulders
4	Side Panels	$^{1}/_{2}$ x $10^{1}/_{2}$ x $12^{15}/_{16}$	$9^{1}/_{2}$ x $11^{15}/_{16}$ exposed
1	Back Panel	$^{13}/_{16}$ x $72^{1}/_{4}$ x $21^{11}/_{16}$	$70^{3}/_{4}$ x $21^{11}/_{16}$ exposed—parts detailed below
1	Back Bottom Rail	$^{13}/_{16}$ x $6^{1}/_{2}$ x $73^{3}/_{4}$	$70^{3}/_{4}$ between tenons
1	Back Top Rail	$^{13}/_{16}$ x $3^{1}/_{4}$ x 67	66 between tenons
2	Back Outer Stiles	$^{13}/_{16}$ x $3^{1}/_{8}$ x $15^{11}/_{16}$	$2^{3}/_{8}$ x $15^{3}/_{16}$ exposed
5	Back Inner Stiles	$^{13}/_{16}$ x $2^{3}/_{4}$ x $12^{15}/_{16}$	$11^{15}/_{16}$ between tongues
6	Back Panels	$^{1}/_{2}$ x 10 x $12^{15}/_{16}$	9 x $11^{15}/_{16}$ exposed
1	Front Rail	$^{13}/_{16}$ x $6^{1}/_{2}$ x $73^{3}/_{4}$	$70^{3}/_{4}$ between tenon shoulders
2	Arms	$^{13}/_{16}$ x $7^{3}/_{4}$ x $36^{3}/_{4}$	
1	Top Cap @ Back	$^{13}/_{16}$ x $7^{3}/_{4}$ x $84^{1}/_{2}$	
6	Corbels	$^{13}/_{16}$ x $3^{1}/_{2}$ x $21^{11}/_{16}$	3 exposed
2	Seat Supports	$^{3}/_{4}$ x $1^{1}/_{2}$ x $70^{3}/_{4}$	
2	Seat Supports	$^{3}/_{4}$ x $1^{1}/_{2}$ x $26^{1}/_{16}$	

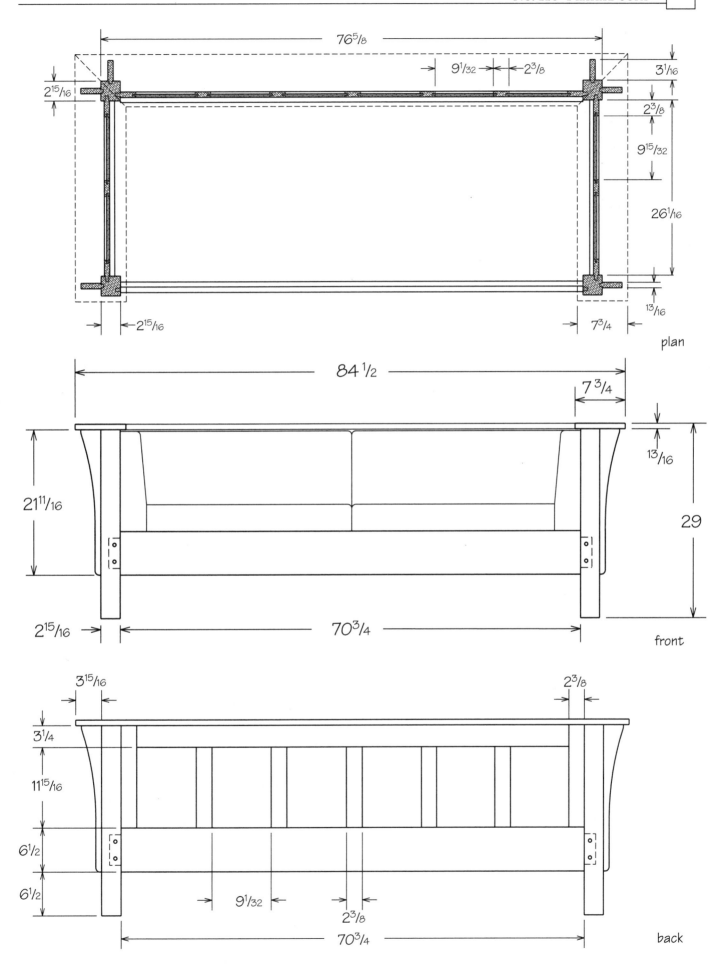

plan

front

back

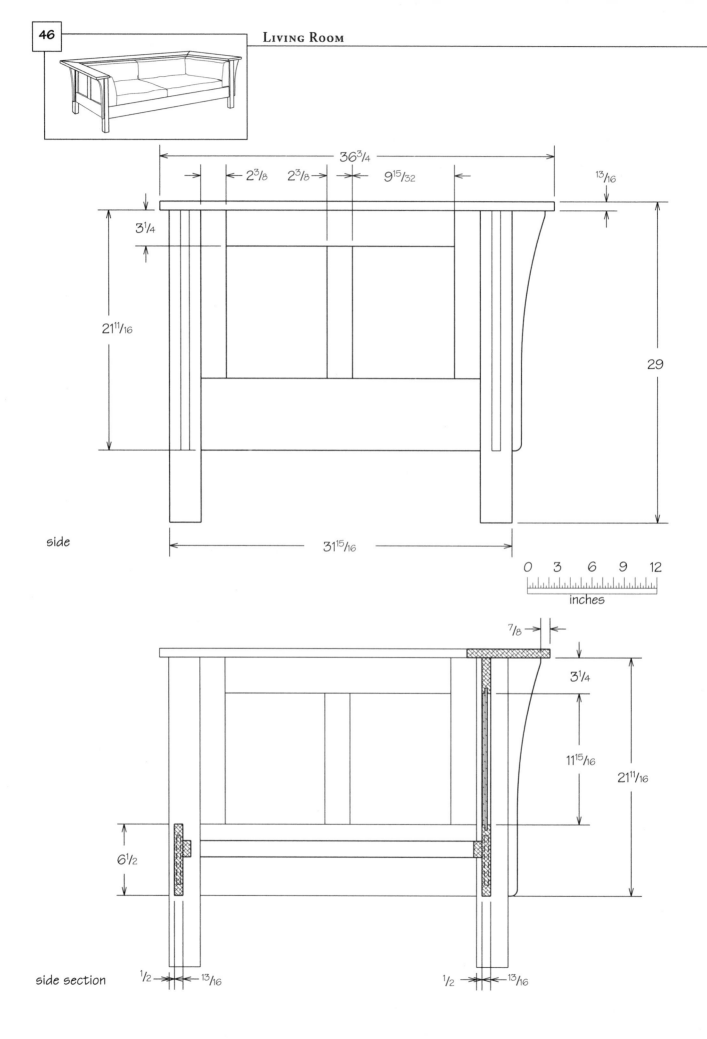

36³/₄

2³/₈   2³/₈   9¹⁵/₃₂

¹³/₁₆

3¹/₄

21¹¹/₁₆

29

side

31¹⁵/₁₆

0   3   6   9   12

inches

⁷/₈

3¹/₄

11¹⁵/₁₆

21¹¹/₁₆

6¹/₂

side section

¹/₂   ¹³/₁₆   ¹/₂   ¹³/₁₆

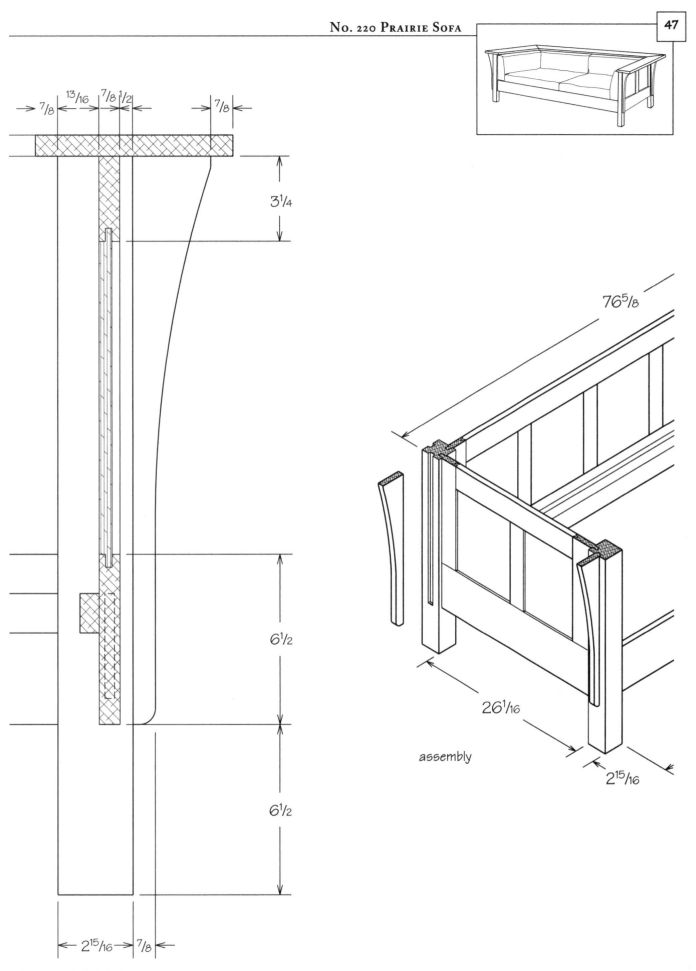

$7/8$ $13/16$ $7/8$ $1/2$ $7/8$

$3^1/4$

$6^1/2$

$6^1/2$

$2^{15}/16$ $7/8$

leg & corbel detail

$76^5/8$

$26^1/16$

$2^{15}/16$

assembly

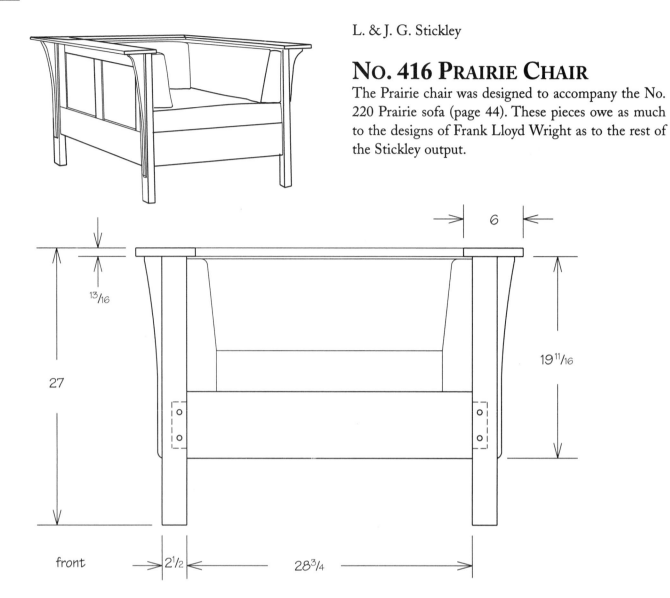

L. & J. G. Stickley

NO. 416 PRAIRIE CHAIR

The Prairie chair was designed to accompany the No. 220 Prairie sofa (page 44). These pieces owe as much to the designs of Frank Lloyd Wright as to the rest of the Stickley output.

L. & J.G. Stickley No. 416 Prairie Chair

QTY.	PART	SIZE	NOTES
4	Legs	$2^{1}/_2$ x $2^{1}/_2$ x $26^{3}/_{16}$	
2	Side Panels	$^{13}/_{16}$ x 28 x $21^{11}/_{16}$	$26^{1}/_2$ x $21^{11}/_{16}$ exposed—parts detailed below
4	Side Outer Stiles	$^{13}/_{16}$ x $3^{1}/_8$ x $15^{11}/_{16}$	$2^{3}/_8$ x $15^{3}/_{16}$ exposed
2	Side Middle Stiles	$^{13}/_{16}$ x $2^{3}/_8$ x $12^{15}/_{16}$	$11^{15}/_{16}$ between tongues
2	Side Top Rails	$^{13}/_{16}$ x $3^{1}/_4$ x $22^{3}/_4$	$21^{3}/_4$ between tongues
2	Side Bottom Rails	$^{13}/_{16}$ x $6^{1}/_2$ x 28	$26^{1}/_2$ between tenon shoulders
4	Side Panels	$^{1}/_2$ x $10^{15}/_{16}$ x $12^{15}/_{16}$	$9^{15}/_{16}$ x $11^{15}/_{16}$ exposed
1	Back Panel	$^{13}/_{16}$ x $30^{1}/_4$ x $21^{11}/_{16}$	$28^{3}/_4$ x $21^{11}/_{16}$ exposed—parts detailed below
1	Back Bottom Rail	$^{13}/_{16}$ x $6^{1}/_2$ x $31^{3}/_4$	$28^{3}/_4$ between tenon shoulders
1	Back Top Rail	$^{13}/_{16}$ x $3^{1}/_4$ x $25^{1}/_2$	24 between tongues
2	Back Outer Stiles	$^{13}/_{16}$ x $3^{1}/_8$ x $15^{11}/_{16}$	$2^{3}/_8$ x $15^{3}/_{16}$ exposed
1	Back Middle Stiles	$^{13}/_{16}$ x $2^{3}/_8$ x $12^{15}/_{16}$	$11^{15}/_{16}$ tongue to tongue
2	Back Panels	$^{1}/_2$ x $11^{13}/_{16}$ x $12^{15}/_{16}$	$10^{13}/_{16}$ x $11^{15}/_{16}$ exposed
1	Front Rail	$^{13}/_{16}$ x $6^{1}/_2$ x $31^{3}/_4$	$28^{3}/_4$ between tenon shoulders
2	Arms	$^{13}/_{16}$ x 6 x 35	
1	Top Cap @ Back	$^{13}/_{16}$ x 6 x 39	
6	Corbels	$^{13}/_{16}$ x $2^{1}/_4$ x $21^{11}/_{16}$	$1^{3}/_4$ exposed
2	Seat Supports	$^{3}/_4$ x $1^{1}/_2$ x $26^{1}/_2$	
2	Seat Supports	$^{3}/_4$ x $1^{1}/_2$ x $28^{3}/_4$	

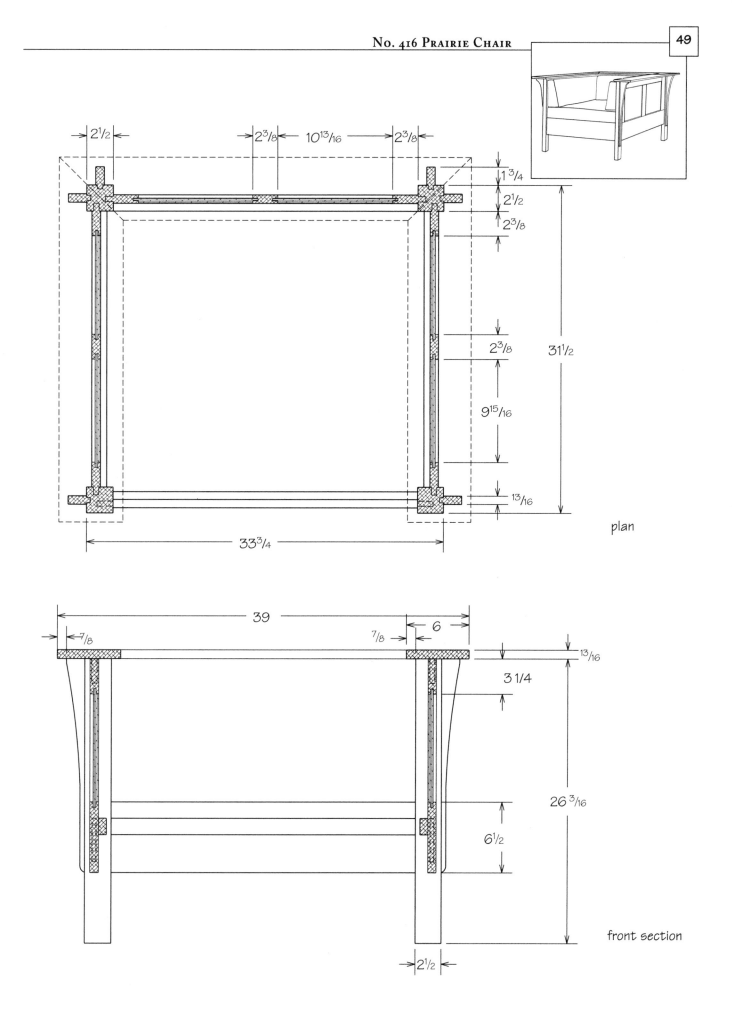

plan

front section

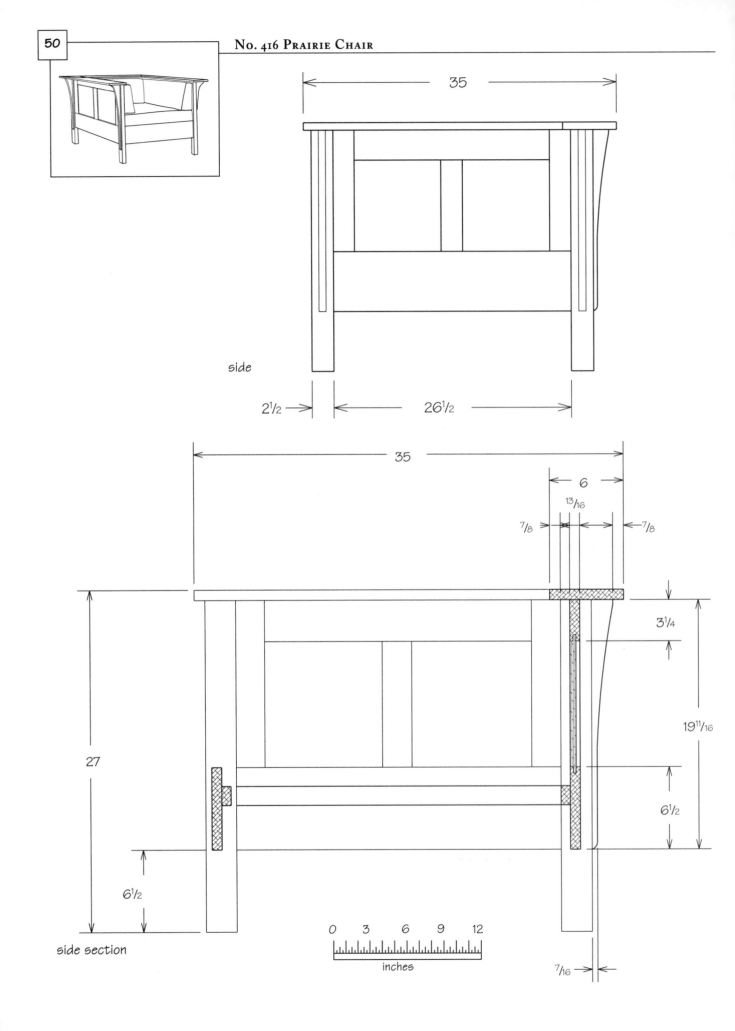

side

35

2½   26½

35

6

¹³/₁₆

⁷/₈   ⁷/₈

3¼

19¹¹/₁₆

27

6½

6½

side section

0   3   6   9   12

inches

⁷/₁₆

L. & J. G. Stickley

No. 516 Table with Open Bookcase
27" x 27" x 29" high

Also known as an encyclopedia table, this is a great place to store a collection of fine books, and a wonderful opportunity for purchasing a hollow-chisel mortiser. When laying out the slats, work from the center out to the ends, and be precise. There are enough slats and spaces for tiny errors to accumulate.

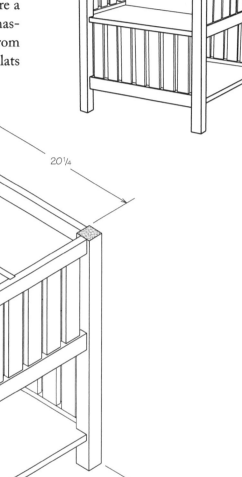

assembly

0 3 6 9 12
inches

L. & J. G. Stickley No.516 Table with Open Bookcase

Qty	Part	Size	Notes
1	Top	$^3/_4$ x 27 x 27	
4	Leg	$1^7/_8$ x $1^7/_8$ x $28^1/_4$	
2	Shelves	$^3/_4$ x 22 x $23^1/_4$	$21^1/_2$ exposed width
1	Upper Vertical Divider	$^3/_4$ x $12^5/_{16}$ x 22	$12^1/_{16}$ x $21^1/_2$ exposed
1	Lower Vertical Divider	$^3/_4$ x $11^7/_{16}$ x 22	$10^{15}/_{16}$ x $21^1/_2$ exposed
2	Top Rails	$^7/_8$ x $1^3/_4$ x $21^1/_2$	$20^1/_4$ between tenon shoulders
4	Mid. & Bot. Rails	$^7/_8$ x 2 x $21^1/_2$	$20^1/_4$ between tenon shoulders
14	Upper Slats	$^5/_8$ x 2 x $10^7/_{16}$	$9^{11}/_{16}$ between tenon shoulders
14	Lower Slats	$^5/_8$ x 2 x $11^1/_{16}$	$10^5/_{16}$ between tenon shoulders

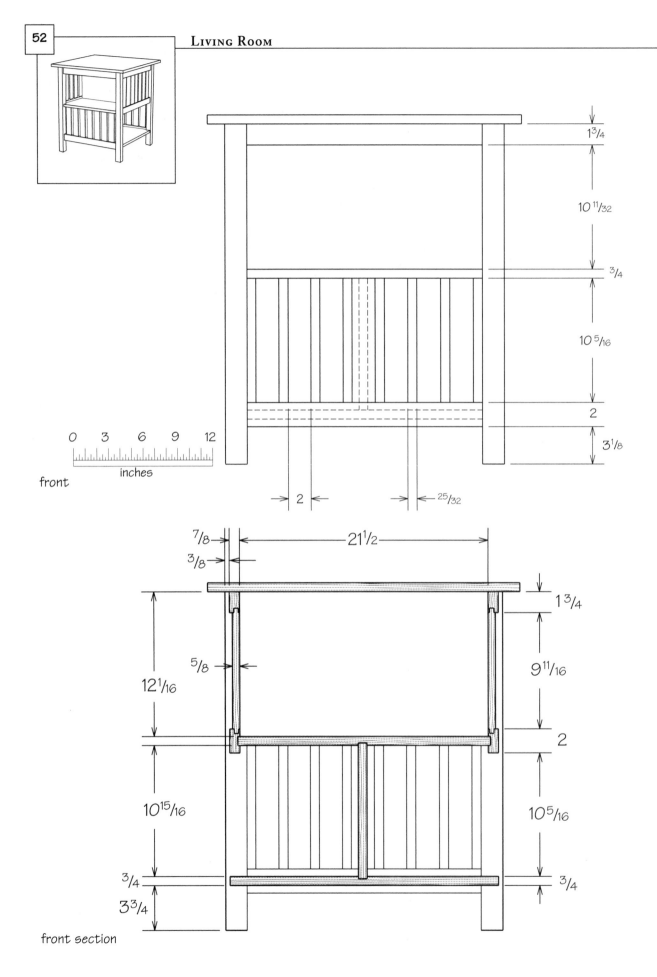

$1^3/4$

$10^{11}/_{32}$

$3/4$

$10^5/_{16}$

2

$3^1/8$

0   3   6   9   12

inches

front

2

$^{25}/_{32}$

$^7/8$

$^3/8$

$21^1/2$

$1^3/4$

$^5/8$

$9^{11}/_{16}$

$12^1/_{16}$

2

$10^{15}/_{16}$

$10^5/_{16}$

$3/4$

$3/4$

$3^3/4$

front section

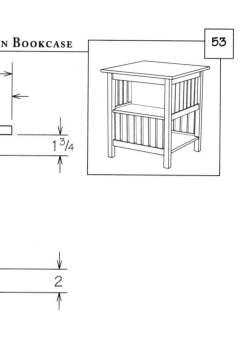

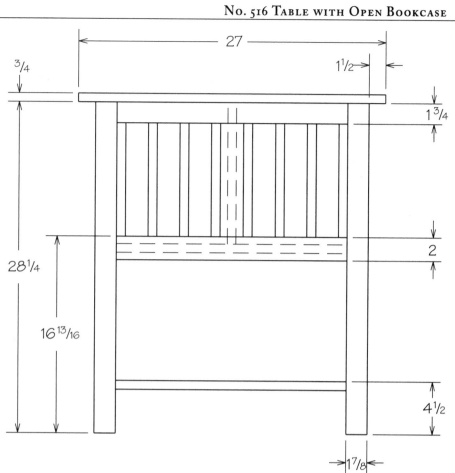

27

3/4

1 1/2

1 3/4

28 1/4

2

16 13/16

4 1/2

side

1 7/8

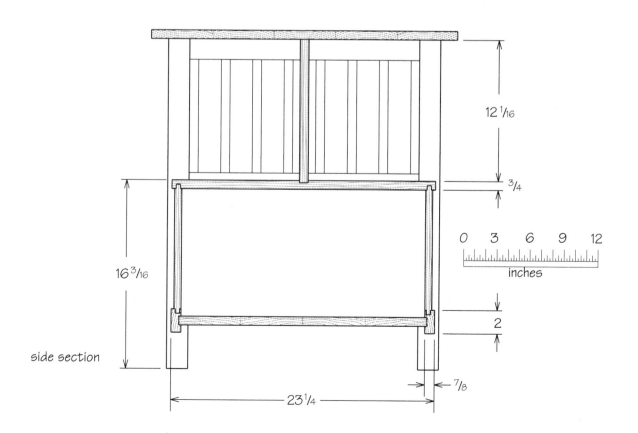

12 1/16

3/4

0   3   6   9   12

inches

16 3/16

2

side section

7/8

23 1/4

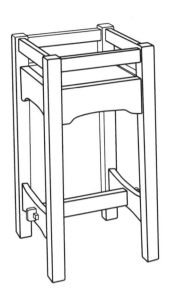

GUSTAV STICKLEY PLANT STAND

26" high x 14" square

The original has a Greuby tile top. If you use tile, finish the stand before setting the tile.

This plan allows for a $\frac{3}{8}$" thick tile. If you use a different thickness, adjust the height of the cleats and plywood accordingly (the top of the tile should be $\frac{1}{8}$" below the adjacent wood).

I couldn't find this plant stand in any of the old catalogs, but at auctions it had a genuine Gustav Stickley tag. L. & J.G. Stickley made a very similar stand, without the arches on the stretchers and without the keyed tenons.

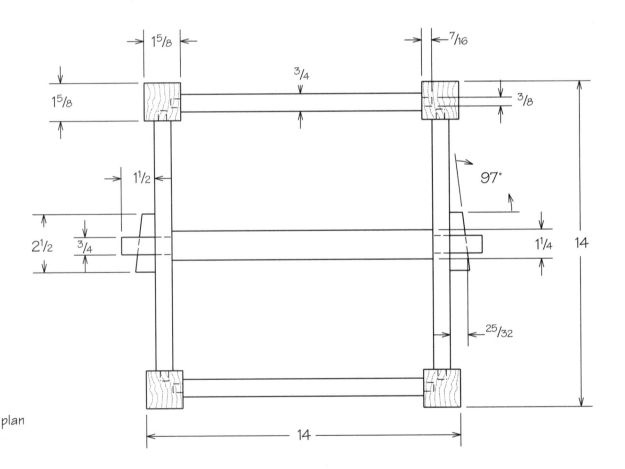

plan

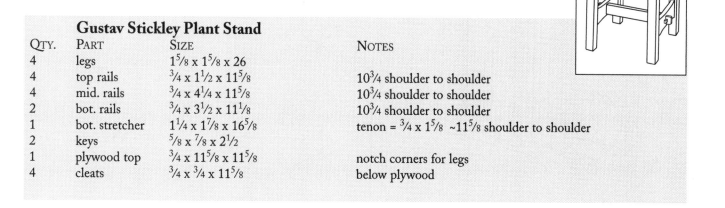

Gustav Stickley Plant Stand

Qty.	Part	Size	Notes
4	legs	$1^5/_8$ x $1^5/_8$ x 26	
4	top rails	$3/_4$ x $1^1/_2$ x $11^5/_8$	$10^3/_4$ shoulder to shoulder
4	mid. rails	$3/_4$ x $4^1/_4$ x $11^5/_8$	$10^3/_4$ shoulder to shoulder
2	bot. rails	$3/_4$ x $3^1/_2$ x $11^1/_8$	$10^3/_4$ shoulder to shoulder
1	bot. stretcher	$1^1/_4$ x $1^7/_8$ x $16^5/_8$	tenon = $3/_4$ x $1^5/_8$ ~$11^5/_8$ shoulder to shoulder
2	keys	$5/_8$ x $7/_8$ x $2^1/_2$	
1	plywood top	$3/_4$ x $11^5/_8$ x $11^5/_8$	notch corners for legs
4	cleats	$3/_4$ x $3/_4$ x $11^5/_8$	below plywood

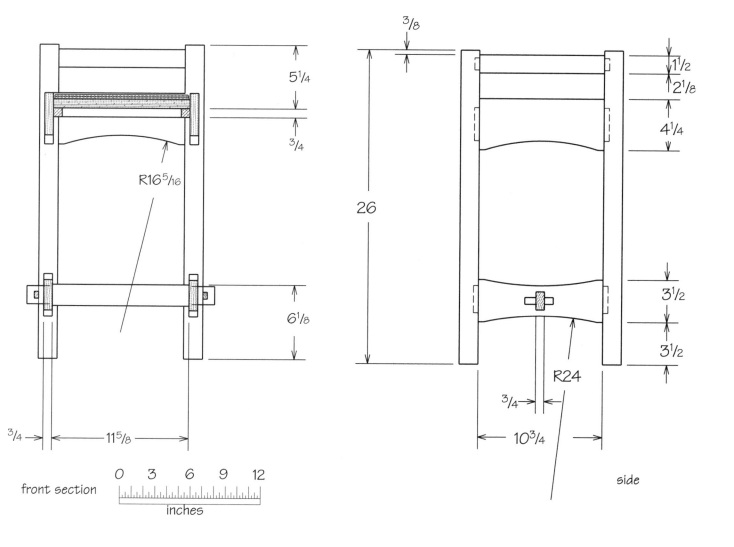

front section

side

0 3 6 9 12

inches

Gustav Stickley

NO. 719 BOOKCASE

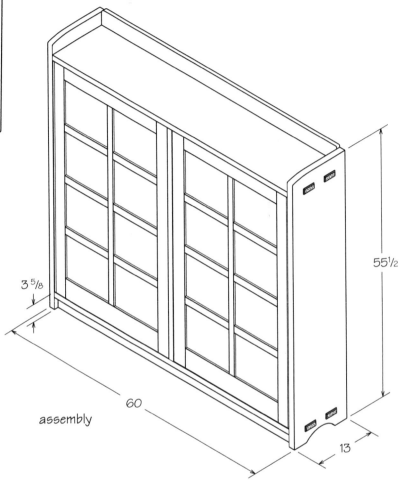

Glass doors are a dust-proof luxury rarely seen on a bookcase today. Though designed as a floor-standing piece, you could mount the case to the wall, and you could use it for curios or china as readily as for books.

3 5/8

55½

assembly

60

13

Gustav Stickley No. 719 Bookcase

QTY	PART	SIZE	NOTES
2	Sides	$1^1/_8$ x 13 x $55^1/_2$	
1	Vertical Divider	$1^1/_8$ x $12^1/_4$ x 48	add to width & length for joints @ bottom & back
6	Adjustable Shelves	$^3/_4$ x $11^3/_{16}$ x $28^3/_{16}$	size is for adjustable shelves—smaller than opening
2	Top & Bottom	$1^1/_8$ x 13 x $60^3/_4$	$57^3/_4$ between tenons—tenons extend beyond sides $^3/_8$
1	Back	$^3/_4$ x 59 x $49^1/_4$	$57^3/_4$ x 48 exposed—shiplap parts listed below
9	Back Planks	$^3/_4$ x $7^3/_{32}$ x $49^1/_4$	will make back $58^{27}/_{32}$ wide—make planks narrower if humid
1	Backsplash	$^3/_4$ x $3^1/_4$ x $57^3/_4$	
1	Toe Board	$^3/_4$ x $2^1/_2$ x $57^3/_4$	
2	Hinge Strips	$^3/_8$ x $^{13}/_{16}$ x 48	
4	Door Stops	$^3/_4$ x $^3/_4$ x $27^{15}/_{16}$	
2	Doors	$^{13}/_{16}$ x $27^{15}/_{16}$ x 48	opening size—trim for desired gaps—parts detailed below
2	Hinge Stiles	$^{13}/_{16}$ x $2^3/_8$ x 48	
2	Middle Stiles	$^{13}/_{16}$ x $2^3/_4$ x 48	
2	Top Door Rails	$^{13}/_{16}$ x $2^3/_4$ x $23^{13}/_{16}$	$22^{13}/_{16}$ between tongues
2	Bot. Door Rails	$^{13}/_{16}$ x $4^1/_8$ x $23^{13}/_{16}$	$22^{13}/_{16}$ between tongues
2	Mullions	$^{13}/_{16}$ x $1^1/_4$ x $42^1/_8$	$41^1/_8$ between tongues
12	Muntins	$^{13}/_{16}$ x $1^1/_2$ x $11^{25}/_{32}$	$10^{25}/_{32}$ between tongues
64LF	Glass Stop	$^1/_4$ x $^1/_4$	

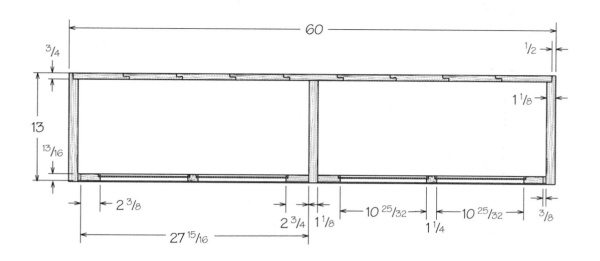

plan

0 3 6 9 12

inches

front

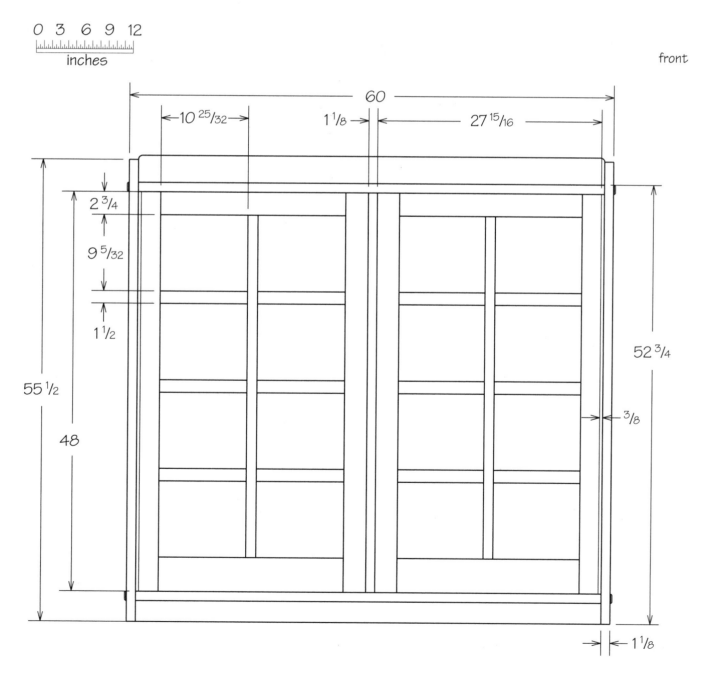

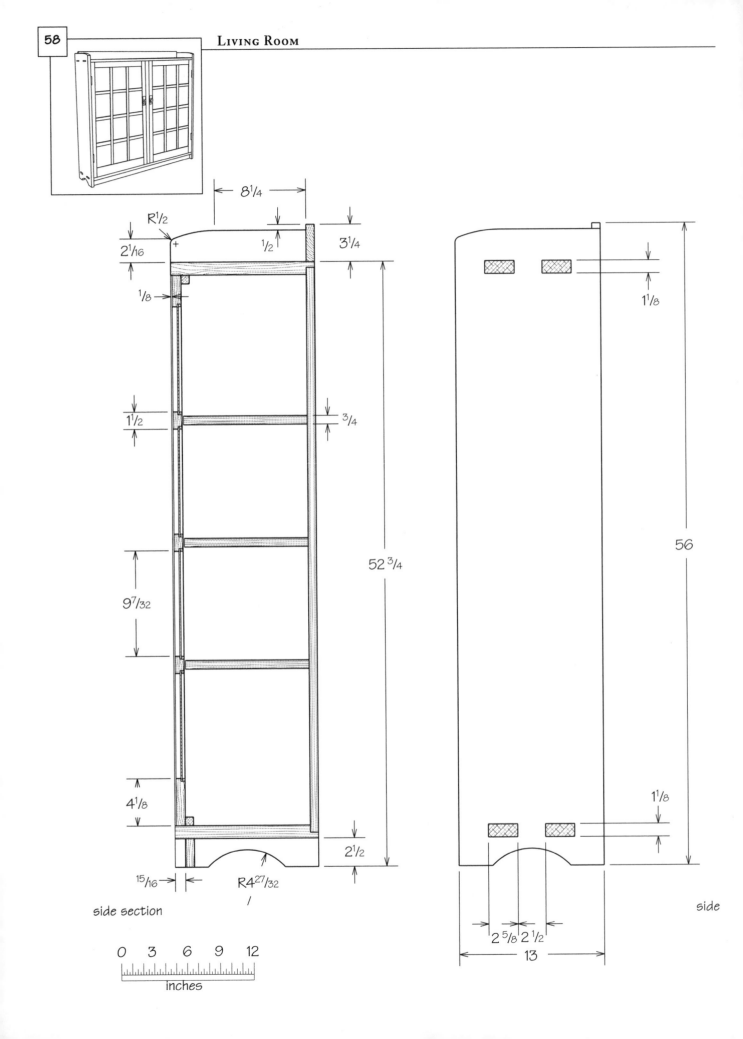

8¹/₄

R¹/₂

2¹/₁₆

¹/₂

3¹/₄

¹/₈

1¹/₂

³/₄

52³/₄

9⁷/₃₂

1¹/₈

56

4¹/₈

2¹/₂

1¹/₈

¹⁵/₁₆

R4²⁷/₃₂

side section

2⁵/₈   2¹/₂

13

side

0   3   6   9   12

inches

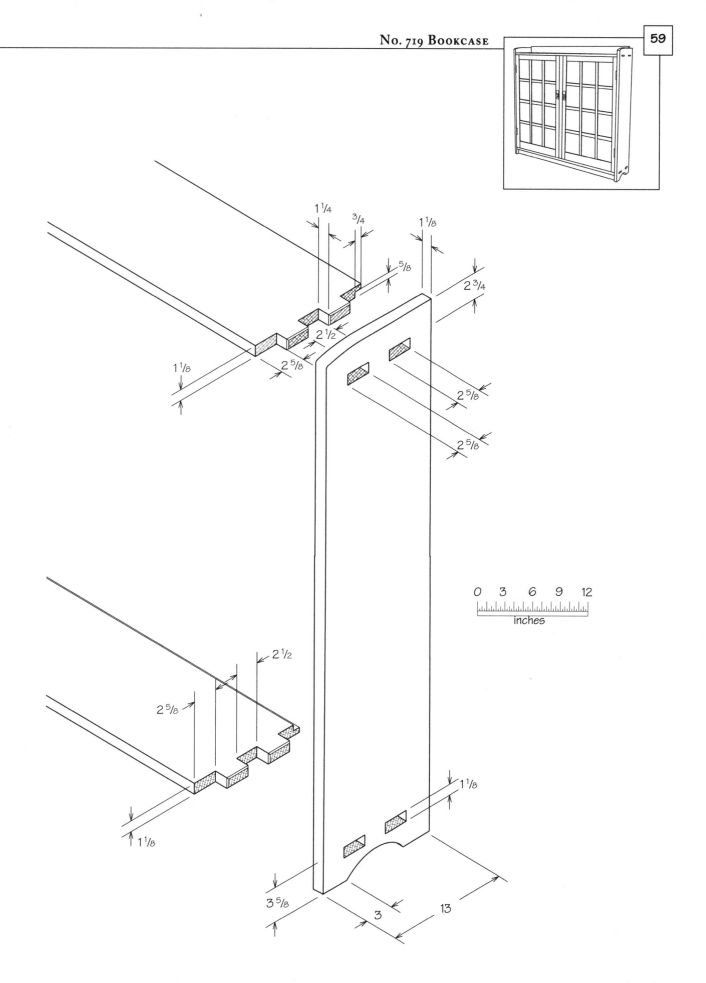

joint detail

Gustav Stickley

NO. 700 BOOKCASE
58" high x 36" wide x 14" deep

One of Harvey Ellis' finest designs. It has a commanding presence even though it is actually rather small.

The original has four panes of leaded glass in each of the top lights. There also was no knob or handle on the original, only a small escutcheon for a key a little more than half-way up the left-hand door stile.

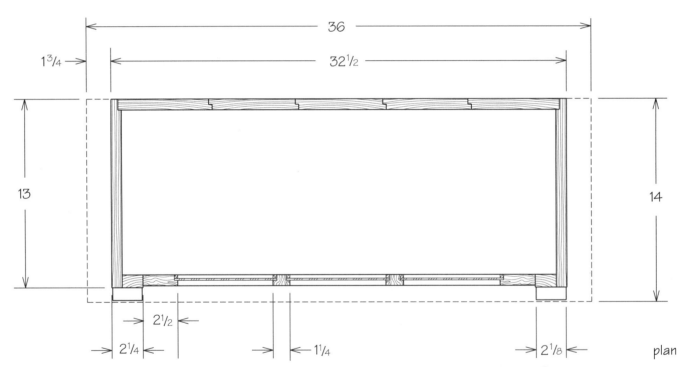

plan

Gustav Stickley No. 700 Bookcase

QTY	PART	SIZE	NOTES
1	Top	$3/4$ x 14 x 36	
2	Sides	$3/4$ x 13 x $57^1/4$	
1	Bottom	$3/4$ x $13^1/2$ x 32	notched @ front of sides, dado into sides, 31 exposed between sides
1	Back	$3/4$ x $31^1/2$ x $51^1/4$	31 exposed between sides, $50^1/2$ exposed between top & bottom
2	Shelves	$3/4$ x $11^1/8$ x $30^7/8$	size for adjustable shelves—smaller than opening
2	Front & Back Toe Boards	$3/4$ x $5^1/16$ x $33^1/4$	31 between tenons—tenons extend $3/8$ beyond sides
2	Stiles	$3/4$ x $1^1/2$ x $50^1/2$	

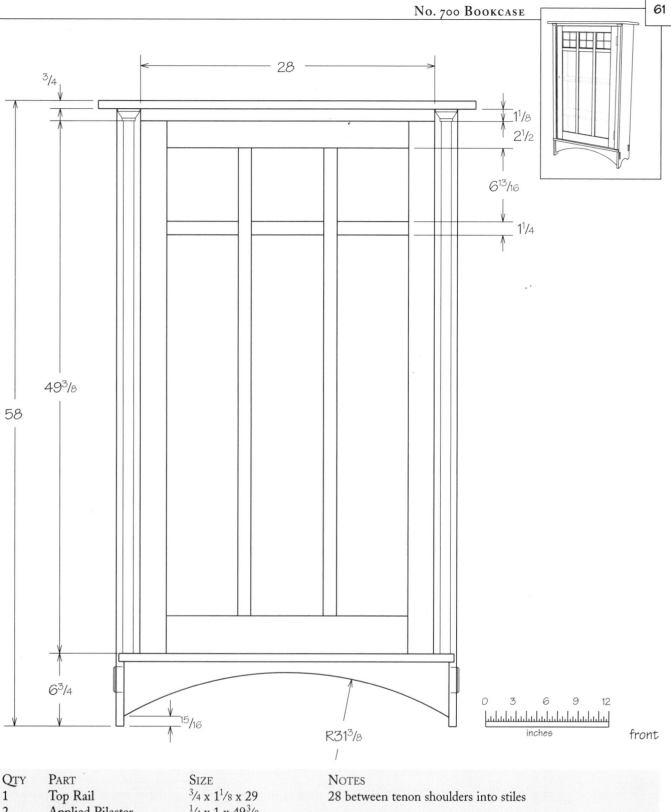

front

QTY	PART	SIZE	NOTES
1	Top Rail	$^3/_4$ x $1^1/_8$ x 29	28 between tenon shoulders into stiles
2	Applied Pilaster	$^1/_4$ x 1 x $49^3/_8$	
2	Pilaster Head Trim Blocks	$^7/_8$ x $2^1/_8$ x $1^1/_8$	see detail
1	Door	$^3/_4$ x 28 x $49^3/_8$	opening size, trim for desired gaps—parts detailed below
2	Door Stiles	$^3/_4$ x $2^1/_2$ x $49^3/_8$	
1	Door Top Rail	$^3/_4$ x $2^1/_2$ x 24	23 between tenon shoulders
1	Door Bottom Rail	$^3/_4$ x $3^1/_2$ x 24	23 between tenon shoulders
2	Mullions	$^3/_4$ x $1^1/_4$ x $44^3/_8$	$43^3/_8$ between tenon shoulders
3	Muntins	$^3/_4$ x $1^1/_4$ x $7^{19}/_{32}$	$6^{27}/_{32}$ between tenon shoulders
32LF	Glass Stop	$^1/_4$ x $^1/_4$	

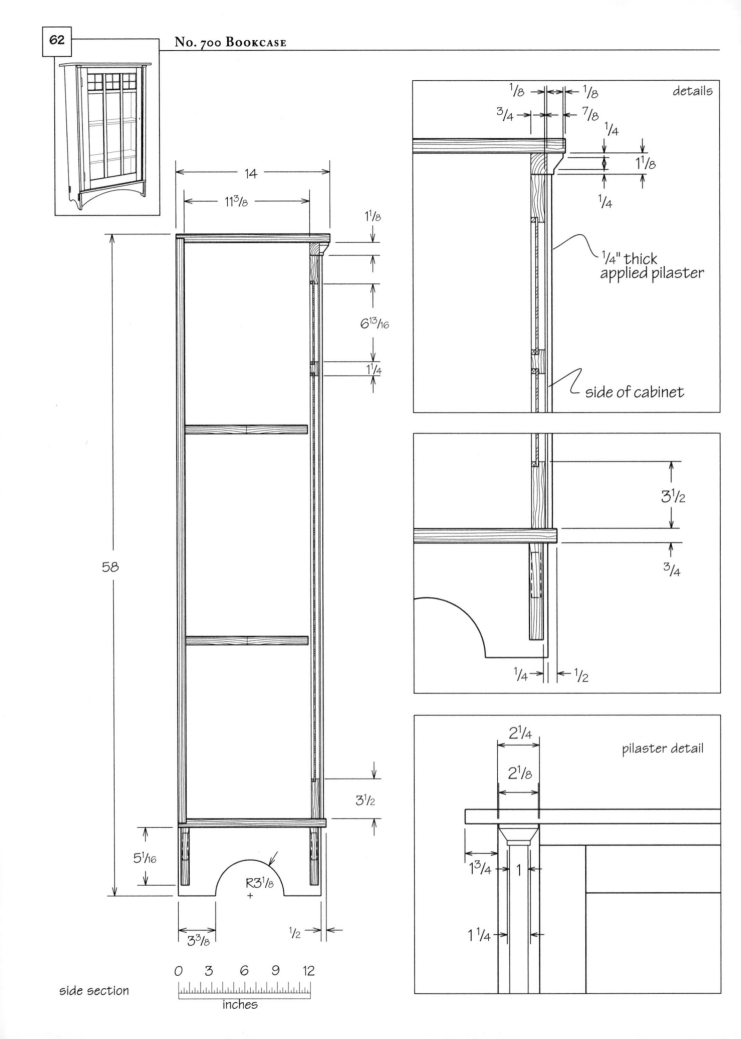

details

$^1/_8$ $^1/_8$

$^3/_4$ $^7/_8$

$^1/_4$

$1^1/_8$

$^1/_4$

$^1/_4$" thick
applied pilaster

side of cabinet

$3^1/_2$

$^3/_4$

$^1/_4$ $^1/_2$

pilaster detail

$2^1/_4$

$2^1/_8$

$1^3/_4$ 1

$1^1/_4$

14

$11^3/_8$

$1^1/_8$

$6^{13}/_{16}$

$1^1/_4$

58

$3^1/_2$

$5^1/_{16}$

$R3^1/_8$
+

$3^3/_8$ $^1/_2$

side section

0 3 6 9 12

inches

Gustav Stickley

No. 332 Morris Chair

A favorite among collectors, this chair is a challenging project. It is also a rewarding project, because once you are finished, you will have the perfect chair to relax in.

Gustav Stickley No. 332 Morris Chair

QTY	PART	SIZE	NOTES
2	Front Legs	$2^7/8$ x $2^7/8$ x $23^1/2$	$22^1/16$ to bottom of arm @ front
2	Rear Legs	$2^7/8$ x $2^7/8$ x $23^1/8$	$21^9/16$ to bottom of arm @ back
			shoulders at tops of legs are angled—do a full size
			layout to determine exact location and angle of legs, arms, slats and side rails
2	Bottom Side Rails	$7/8$ x $4^7/8$ x 25	$18^1/4$ tenon to tenon—tenons are at an angle—do full size layout
10	Side Slats	$5/8$ x 3 x 18*	
2	Arms	$1^1/8$ x $6^3/8$ x 35	
1	Front Rail	$7/8$ x $5^1/8$ x $33^3/4$	27 between tenon shoulders
1	Back Rail	$7/8$ x $5^1/8$ x $33^3/4$	27 between tenons—angle on top edge
2	Back Uprights	$1^1/2$ x $1^1/2$ x 31	
1	Back Top Slat-curved	$3/4$ x $3^1/4$ x 30*	23 between tenons, bent to 36" inside radius, make long for bending
4	Back Mid. Slats-curved	$3/4$ x 3 x 30*	23 between tenons, bent to 36 inside radius—make long for bending
1	Back Bot. Slat	$15/16$ x $2^{13}/32$ x 30*	23 between tenons, bent to 36 inside radius—make long for bending
4	Pegs	1 x 1 x $4^3/16$	turn post slightly less than $5/8$ diameter x $2^1/2$ long
2	Washers	$1/4$ thick x $1^1/2$ diameter	$5/8$ hole between back and rear legs

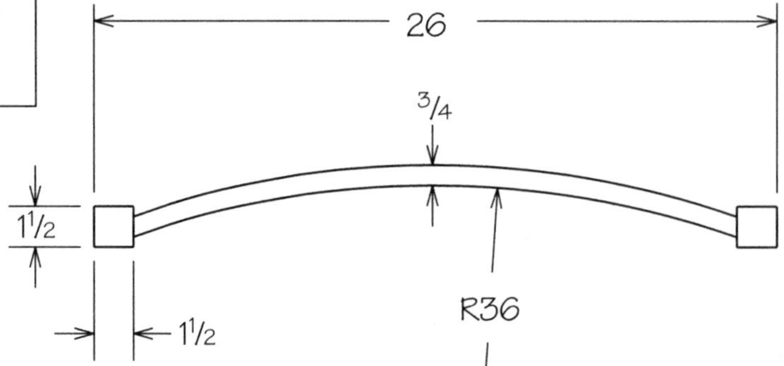

26

3/4

1 1/2

1 1/2

R36

"true" plan of back

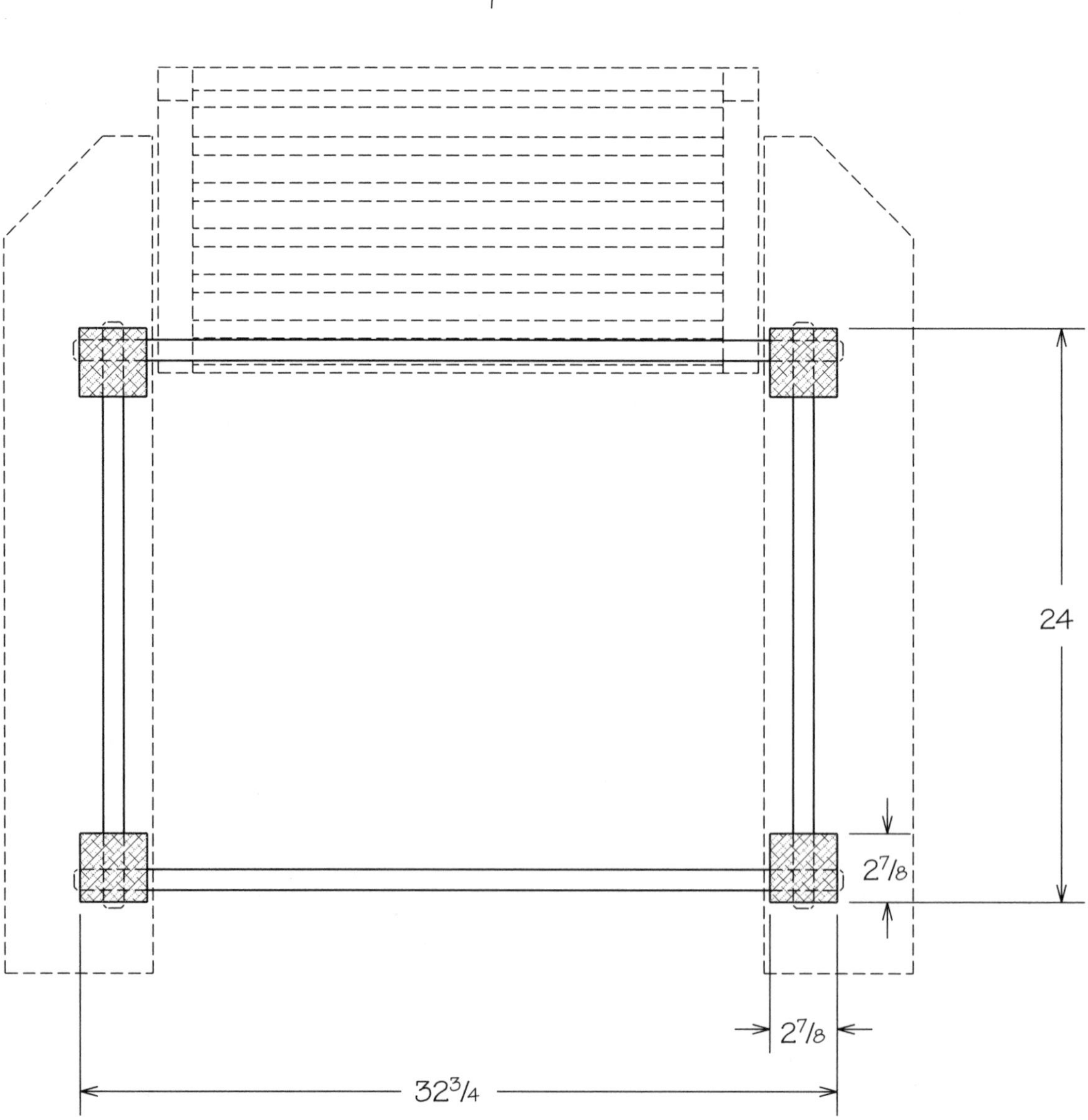

24

2 7/8

2 7/8

32 3/4

plan

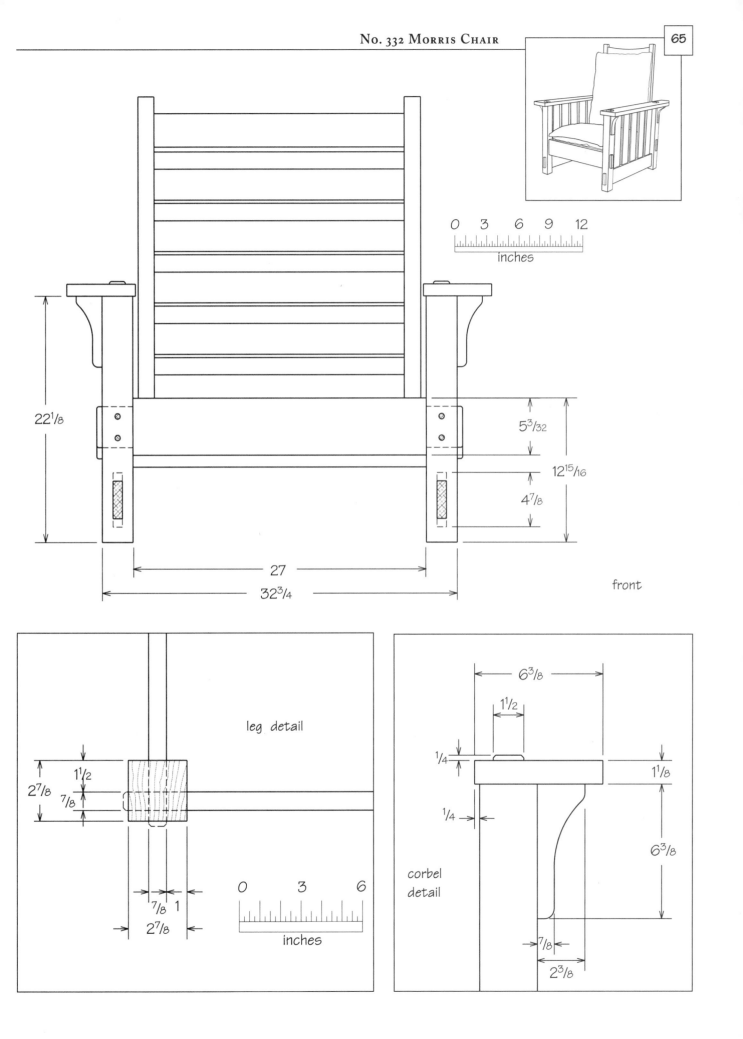

0 3 6 9 12

inches

$22^1/8$

$5^3/32$

$12^{15}/16$

$4^7/8$

27

$32^3/4$

front

leg detail

$1^1/2$

$2^7/8$

$7/8$

$7/8$ 1

$2^7/8$

0 3 6

inches

$6^3/8$

$1^1/2$

$1/4$

$1^1/8$

$1/4$

$6^3/8$

corbel
detail

$7/8$

$2^3/8$

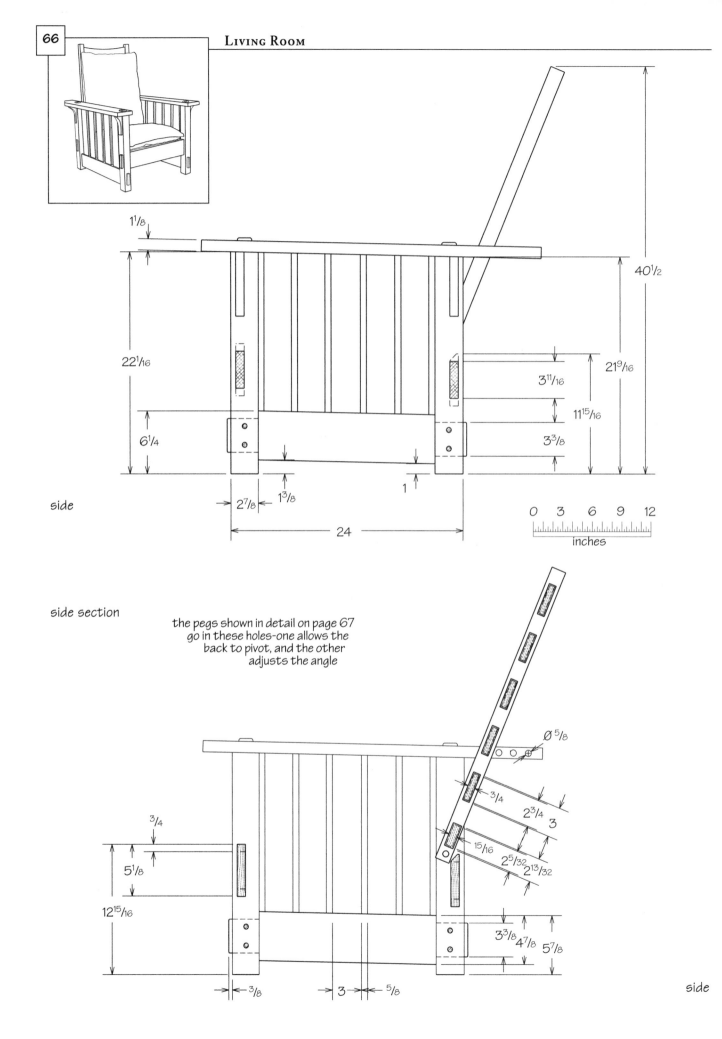

1¹/₈

40¹/₂

22¹/₁₆

21⁹/₁₆

3¹¹/₁₆

11¹⁵/₁₆

6¹/₄

3³/₈

1

side

2⁷/₈   1³/₈

24

0   3   6   9   12
inches

side section

the pegs shown in detail on page 67
go in these holes-one allows the
back to pivot, and the other
adjusts the angle

Ø ⁵/₈

³/₄

³/₄

2³/₄

3

5¹/₈

¹⁵/₁₆

2⁵/₃₂   2¹³/₃₂

12¹⁵/₁₆

3³/₈   4⁷/₈   5⁷/₈

³/₈   3   ⁵/₈

side

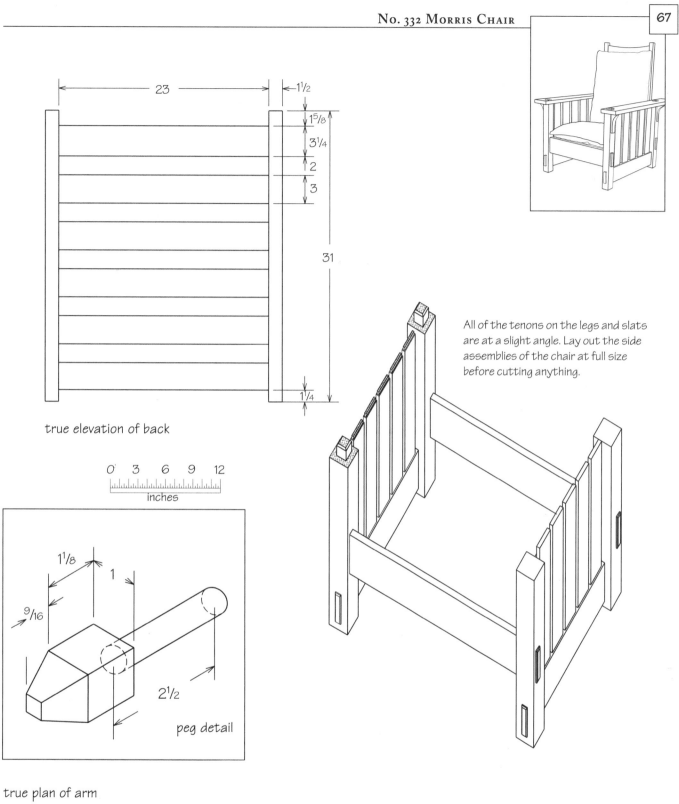

23 ←1½

1½
1⁵/₈
3¼
2
3
31
1¼

true elevation of back

0 3 6 9 12
inches

All of the tenons on the legs and slats are at a slight angle. Lay out the side assemblies of the chair at full size before cutting anything.

1⅛
1
⁹/₁₆
2½

peg detail

true plan of arm

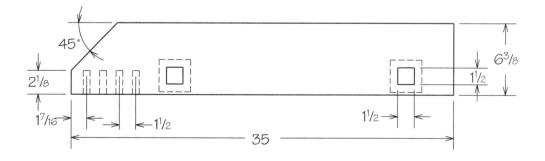

45°

2⅛

1⁷/₁₆

6³/₈

1½

1½

1½

35

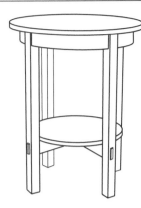

L. & J.G. Stickley

No. 540 Occasional Table

24" dia. x 30" high

Most of the original versions of this type of table had the curved aprons cut from solid stock, leaving very weak short grain where the aprons join the legs. In most of the examples I have seen this joint has failed, with the wood at the end of the apron actually falling apart. A better approach would be to make the aprons from curved plywood, or to laminate them from several thin, solid-wood strips.

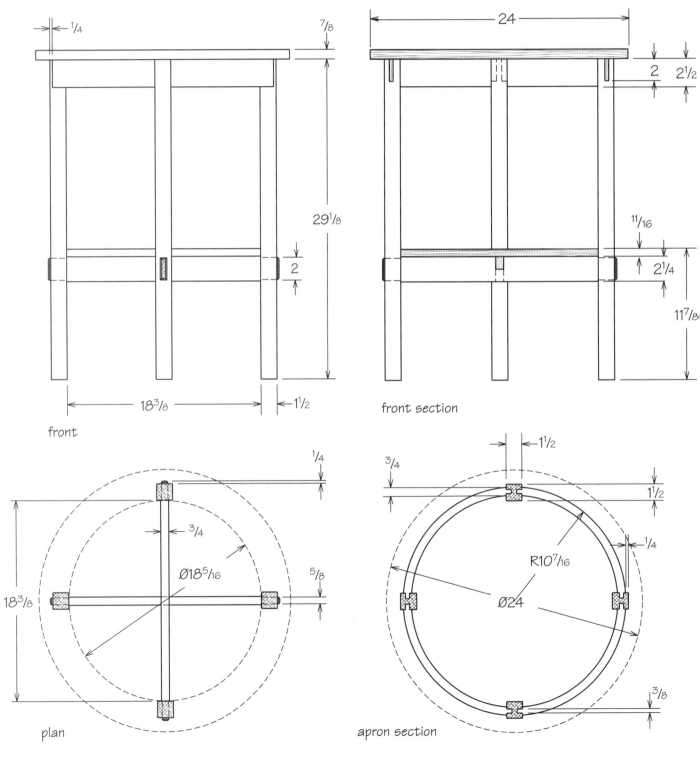

assembly

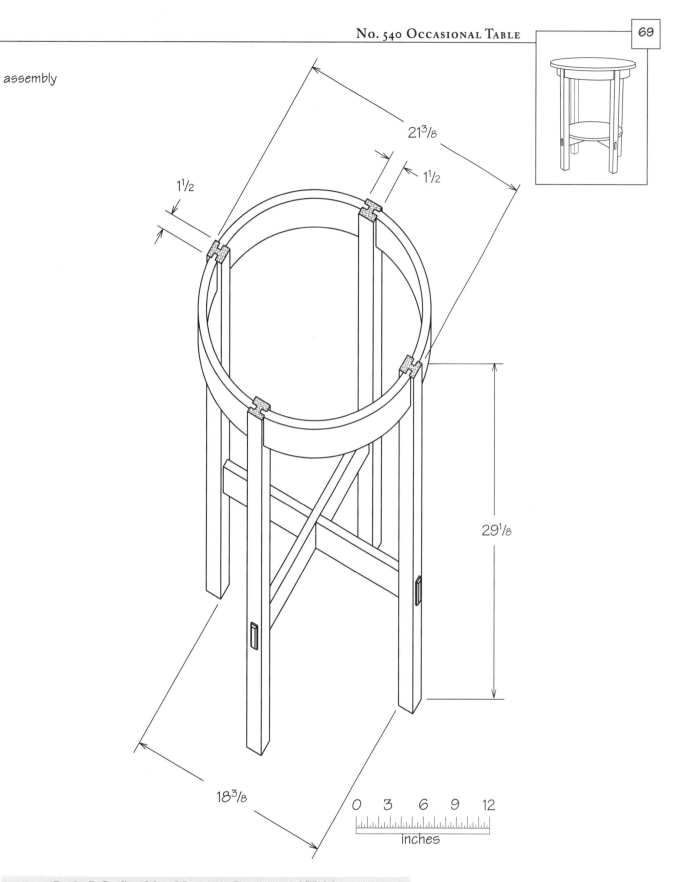

21³/₈

1¹/₂

1¹/₂

29¹/₈

18³/₈

0   3   6   9   12
inches

	L. & J.G. Stickley No. 540 Occasional Table		
QTY	PART	SIZE	NOTES
1	Top	⁷/₈ x 24 diameter	
1	Shelf	³/₄ x 18⁵/₁₆ dia.	
4	Legs	1¹/₂ x 1¹/₂ x	Curved
4	Bot. Stretchers	³/₄ x 2¹/₄ x 21⁷/₈	18³/₈ between tenons

FOYER
& DEN

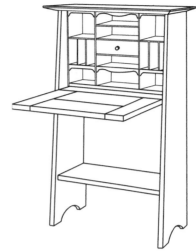

No. 706 Drop-Front Desk
page 82

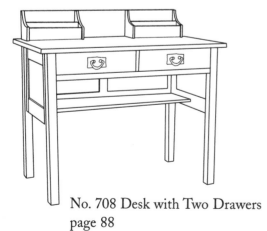

No. 216 Settle
page 76

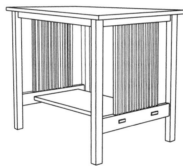

No. 655 Library Table
page 79

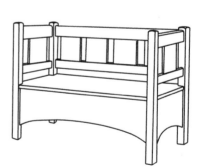

No. 207 Settle
page 72

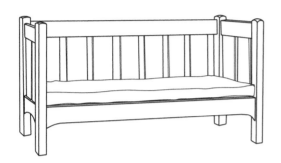

No. 708 Desk with Two Drawers
page 88

Roycroft "Little Journeys"
Book Stand   page 93

L. & J. G. Stickley

NO. 207 SETTLE
32" high x 42" wide x 18" deep

Note that the tenons on the rails are offset. This allows them to be long enough to accept a peg through the joint. The seat is hinged at the back to allow access to the storage space beneath.

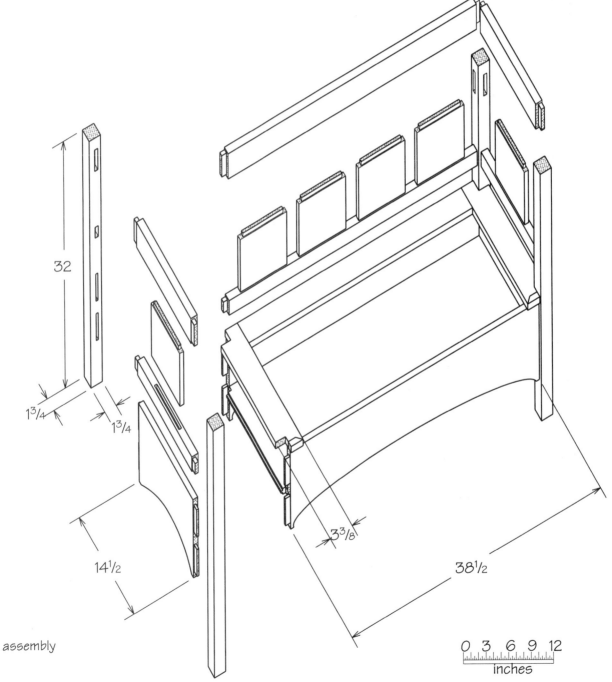

32

1³/₄

1³/₄

14¹/₂

3³/₈

38¹/₂

assembly

0 3 6 9 12
inches

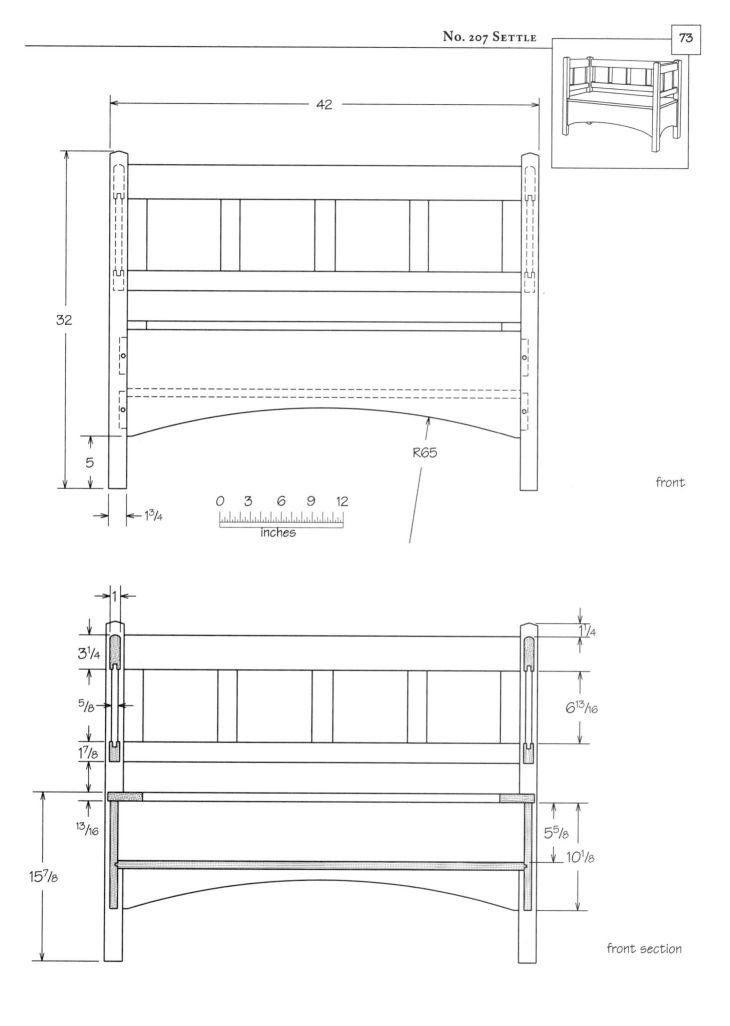

42

32

5

1³/₄

0 3 6 9 12
inches

R65

front

1

3¹/₄

⁵/₈

1⁷/₈

¹³/₁₆

15⁷/₈

1¹/₄

6¹³/₁₆

5⁵/₈

10¹/₈

front section

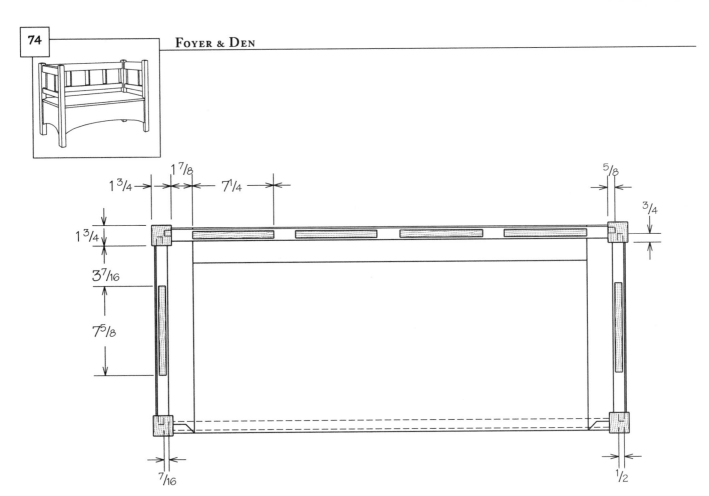

section above seat

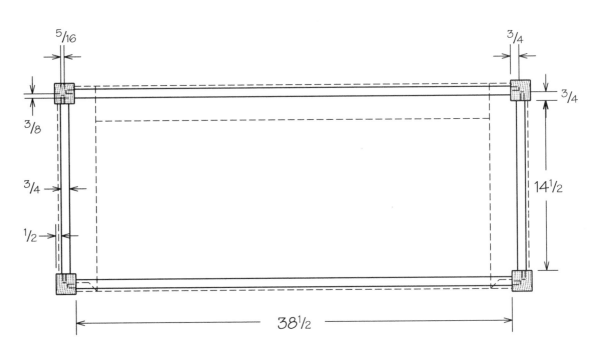

section below seat

L. & J.G. Stickley No. 207 Settle

QTY	PART	SIZE	NOTES
4	Legs	$1^3/_4$ x $1^3/_4$ x 32	
1	Top Back Rail	1 x $3^1/_4$ x $39^3/_4$	$38^1/_2$ between tenon shoulders
1	Bot. Back Rail	1 x $1^7/_8$ x $39^3/_4$	$38^1/_2$ between tenon shoulders
4	Back Slats	$5/_8$ x $7^1/_4$ x $7^{13}/_{16}$	$6^{13}/_{16}$ between tenon shoulders
2	Top Side Rails	1 x $3^1/_4$ x 16	$14^1/_2$ between tenon shoulders
2	Bot. Side Rails	1 x $1^7/_8$ x 16	$14^1/_2$ between tenon shoulders
2	Side Slats	$5/_8$ x $7^5/_8$ x $7^{13}/_{16}$	$6^{13}/_{16}$ between tenon shoulders
2	Arched Sides Below Seat	$3/_4$ x $10^1/_8$ x 16	$14^1/_2$ between tenon shoulders
2	Arched Front & Back Below Seat	$3/_4$ x $10^1/_8$ x 40	$38^1/_2$ between tenon shoulders
2	Seat Stiles	$3/_4$ x $3^3/_8$ x $17^1/_2$	notch @ legs, mitered return @ front
1	Seat	$3/_4$ x $14^1/_2$ x $34^3/_4$	opening size—trim for desired gaps
1	Bottom Below Seat	$3/_4$ x 16 x 40	$15^1/_2$ x $39^1/_2$ exposed between tongues

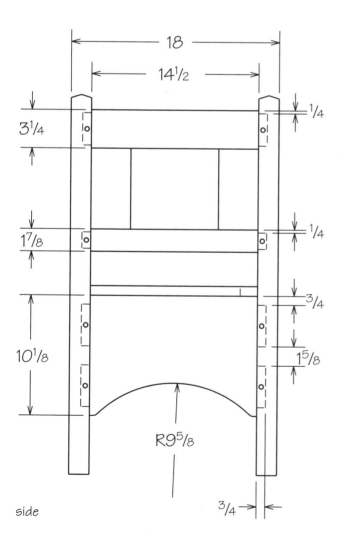

side

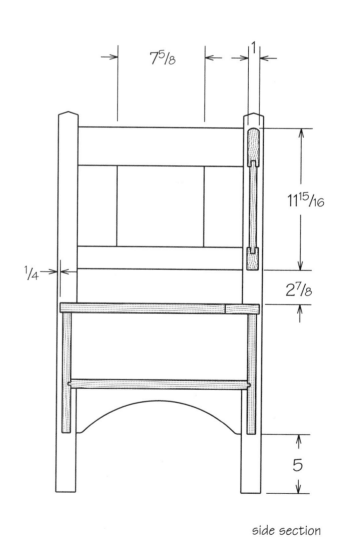

side section

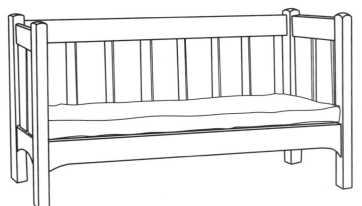

L. & J. G. Stickley

NO. 216 SETTLE

72" wide x 26" deep x 36" high

The original had a spring support for the cushion. The modern, easy way out is to have a futon mattress made to the appropriate size, and support it with wooden slats running from front to back.

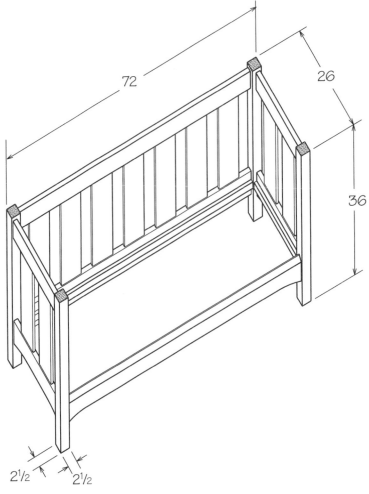

L. & J.G. Stickley No. 216 Settle

QTY	PART	SIZE	NOTES
4	Legs	$2^1/_2$ x $2^1/_2$ x 36	
1	Top Back Rail	$1^1/_8$ x 4 x 69	67 between tenon shoulders
1	Bottom Back Rail	$1^1/_8$ x $4^1/_2$ x 69	67 between tenon shoulders
7	Back Slats	$5/_8$ x $5^3/_4$ x $20^7/_8$	$19^7/_8$ between tenon shoulders
1	Front Rail	$1^1/_8$ x $5^1/_2$ x 69	67 between tenon shoulders
2	Top Side Rails	$1^1/_8$ x 4 x 24	21 between tenon shoulders
2	Bottom Side Rails	$1^1/_8$ x $4^1/_2$ x 24	21 between tenon shoulders
2	Side Slats	$5/_8$ x $5^3/_4$ x $20^7/_8$	$19^7/_8$ between tenon shoulders
2	Seat Supports	$3/_4$ x $1^1/_2$ x 67	
2	Seat Supports	$3/_4$ x $1^1/_2$ x 21	

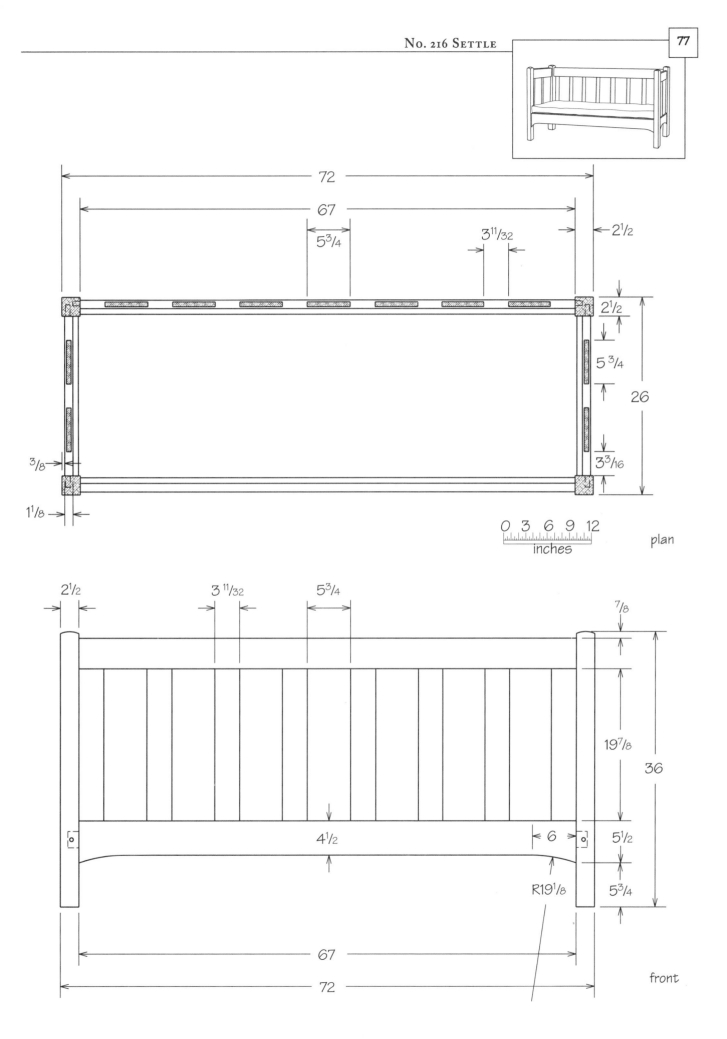

72

67

$5^3/4$

$3^{11}/32$

$2^1/2$

$2^1/2$

$5^3/4$

26

$3^3/16$

$3/8$

$1^1/8$

0 3 6 9 12

inches

plan

$2^1/2$

$3^{11}/32$

$5^3/4$

$7/8$

$19^7/8$

36

$4^1/2$

6

$5^1/2$

$R19^1/8$

$5^3/4$

67

72

front

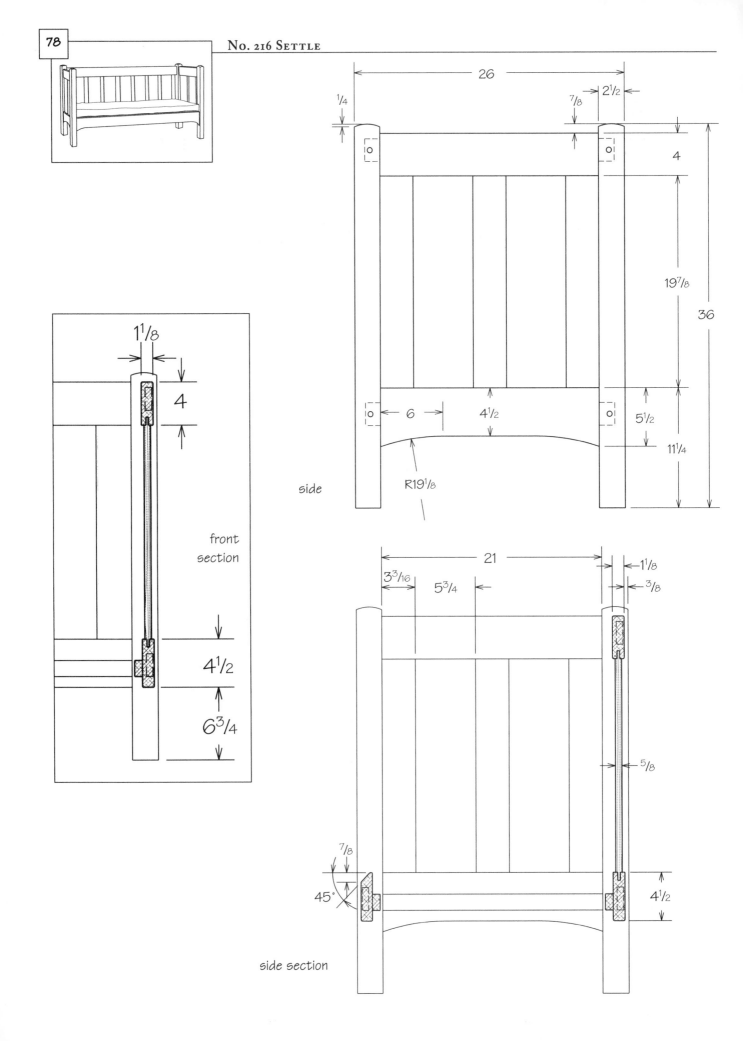

26

1/4

7/8   2½

4

19⁷/₈

36

side

6   4½

5½

11¼

R19¹/₈

1¹/₈

4

front
section

4¹/₂

6³/₄

21

3³/₁₆   5³/₄

1¹/₈

3/8

5/8

7/8

45°

4¹/₂

side section

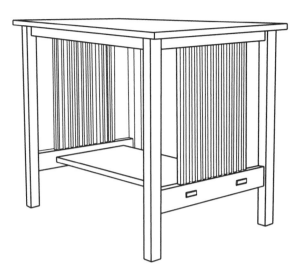

Gustav Stickley

No. 655 Library Table
29" high x 48" wide x 30" deep

The 655 library table would be an elegant addition to your library, if you had one, and if you added a keyboard tray, an excellent computer desk in the Arts & Crafts style.

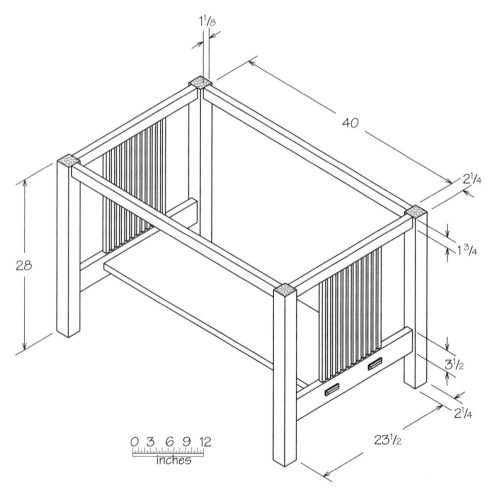

assembly

Gustav Stickley No. 655 Library Table			
Qty	Part	Size	Notes
1	Top	1 x 30 x 48	
4	Legs	$2^{1}/_{4}$ x $2^{1}/_{4}$ x 28	
2	Long Top Rails	$1^{1}/_{8}$ x $1^{3}/_{4}$ x $41^{1}/_{2}$	40 between tenon shoulders
2	Short top Rails	$1^{1}/_{8}$ x $1^{3}/_{4}$ x 25	$23^{1}/_{2}$ between tenon shoulders
2	Bottom Rails	$1^{1}/_{8}$ x $3^{1}/_{4}$ x 25	$23^{1}/_{2}$ between tenon shoulders
1	Shelf	1 x 13 x $44^{1}/_{8}$	$41^{1}/_{8}$ between tenon shoulders
24	Spindles	$^{5}/_{8}$ x $^{5}/_{8}$ x $18^{7}/_{8}$	$18^{1}/_{8}$ between tenon shoulders

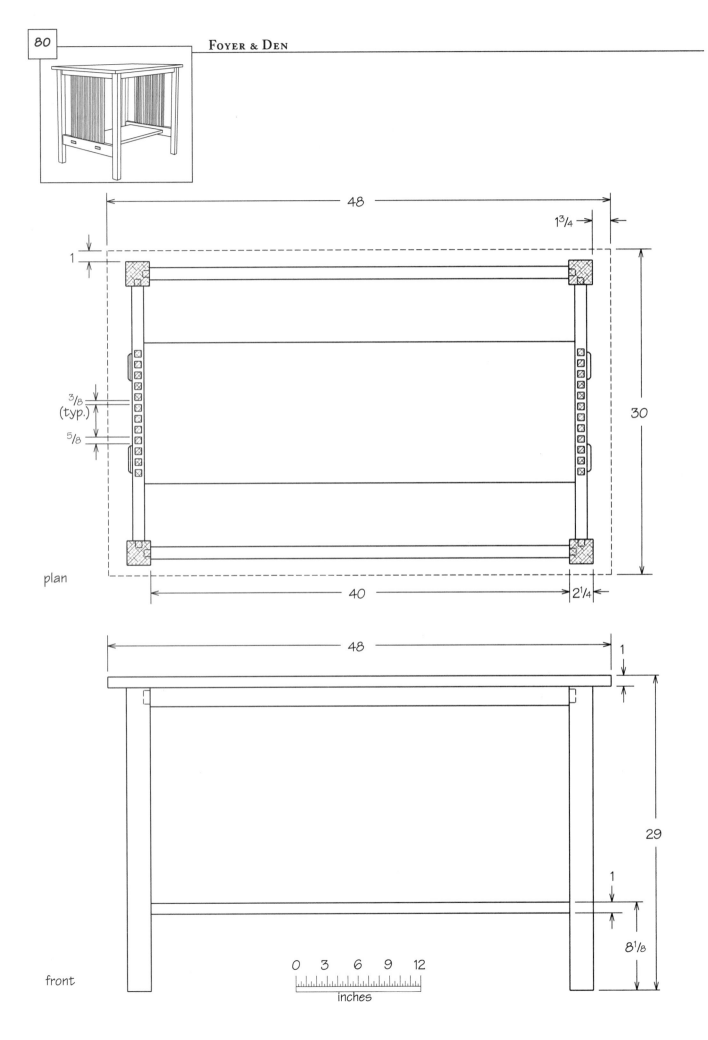

plan

48

1³/₄

1

30

³/₈ (typ.)

⁵/₈

40

2¹/₄

48

1

29

1

8¹/₈

front

0   3   6   9   12

inches

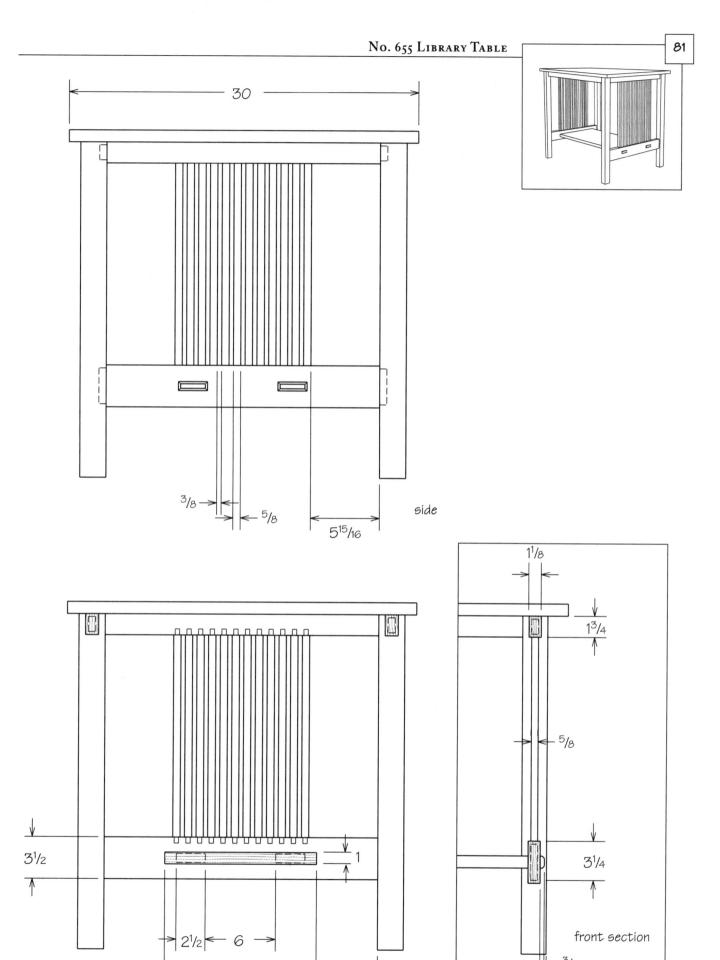

30

side

3/8

5/8

5¹⁵/16

1¹/8

1³/4

5/8

3¹/4

front section

3/8

3¹/2

1

2¹/2

6

13

5¹/4

side section

Gustav Stickley

No. 706
DROP-FRONT DESK
44" high x 30" wide x 11" deep

This is truly an elegant little desk, and a challenge to build.

Make the pigeonholes as a separate section, and secure that with screws to the sides of the cabinet. The writing surface can be hinged with pivot hinges. Locate them so that when opened, this surface stops against the bottom of the pigeonhole insert.

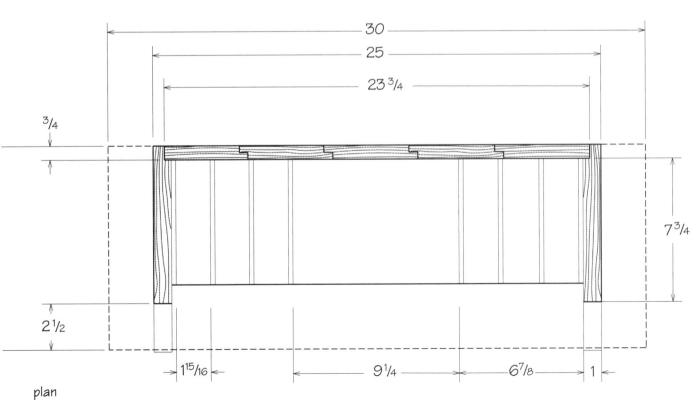

plan

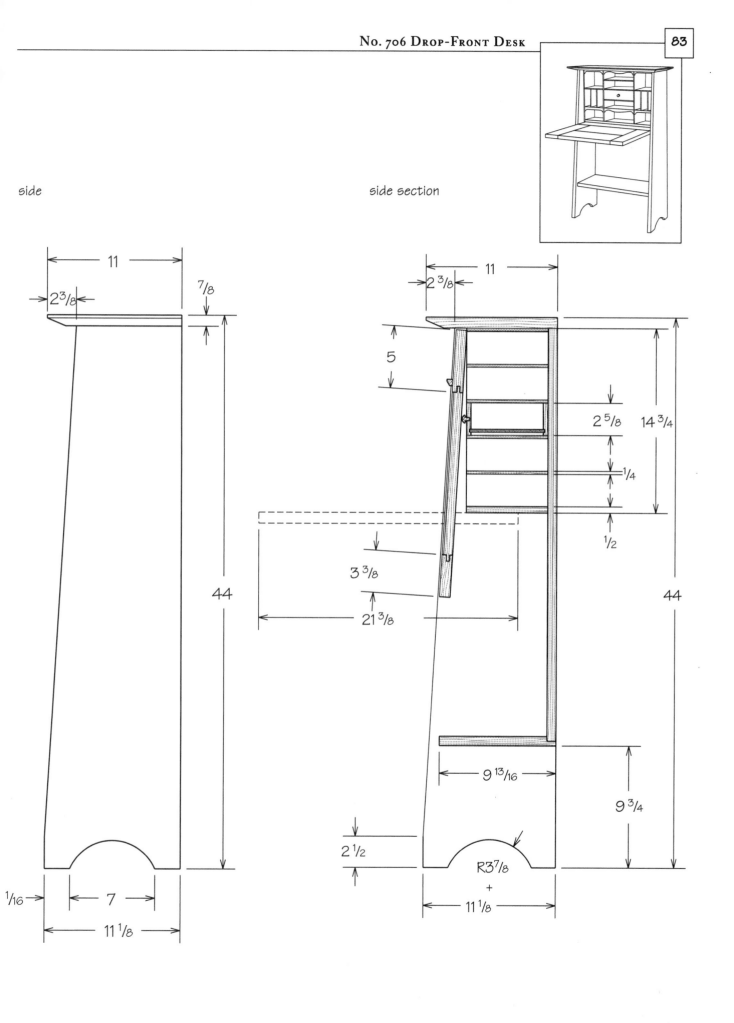

side

side section

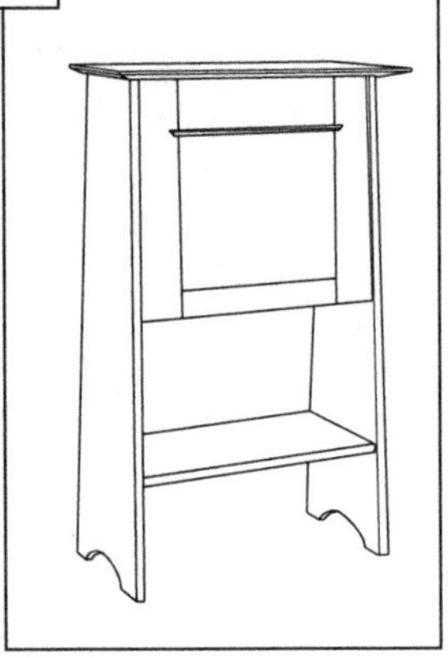

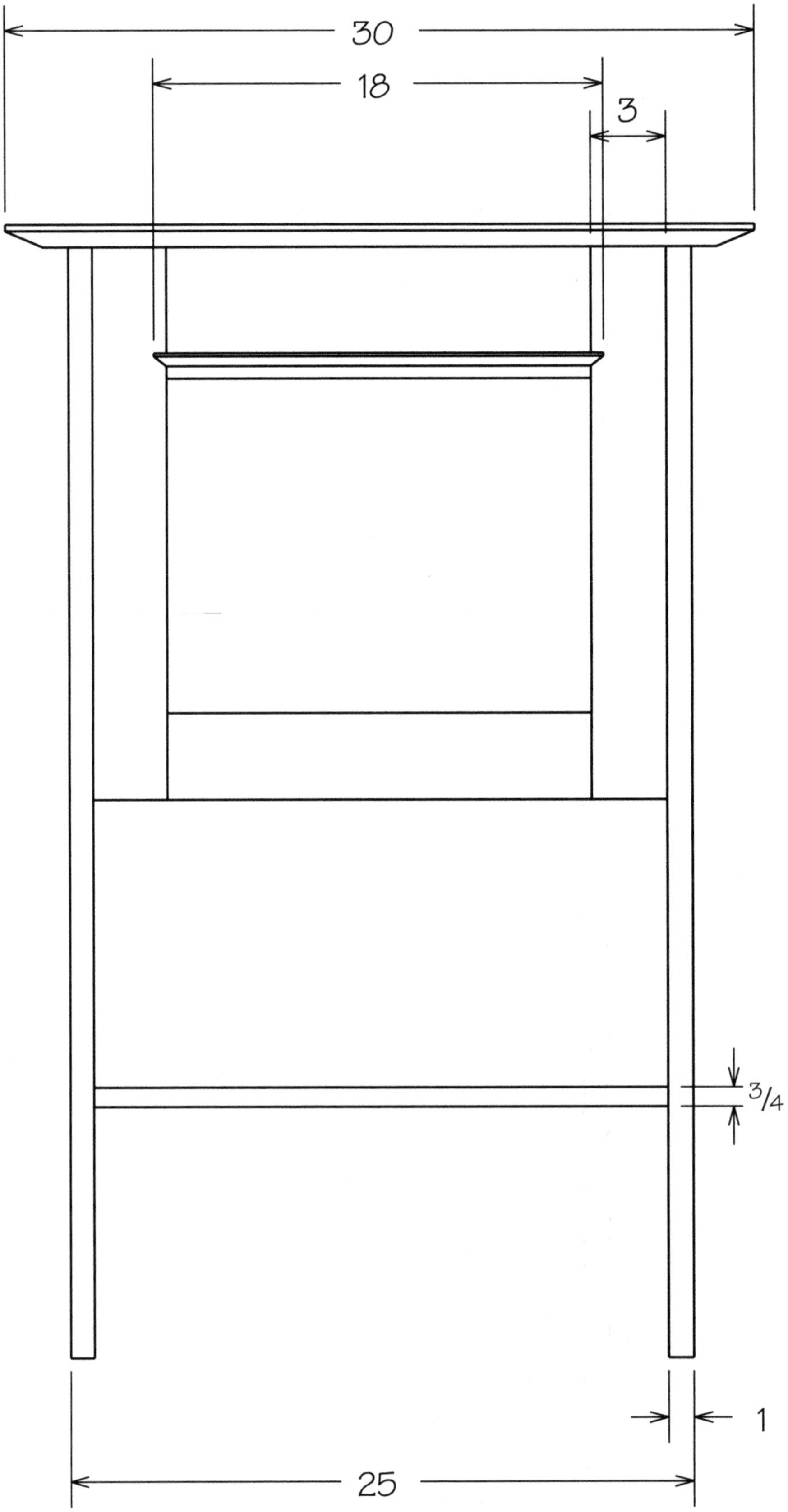

30

18

3

3/4

front closed

1

25

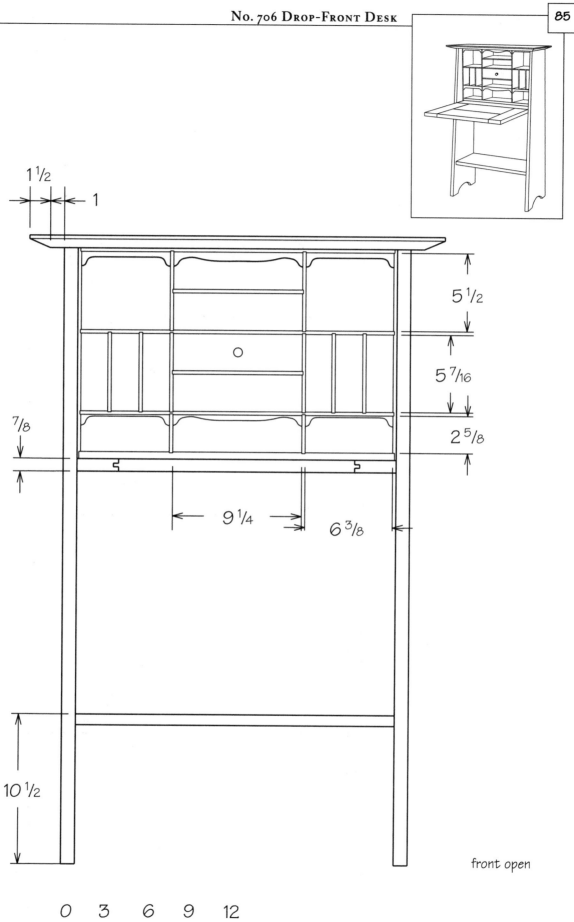

$1^1/_2$

1

$5^1/_2$

$5^7/_{16}$

$2^5/_8$

$^7/_8$

$9^1/_4$

$6^3/_8$

$10^1/_2$

front open

0   3   6   9   12

inches

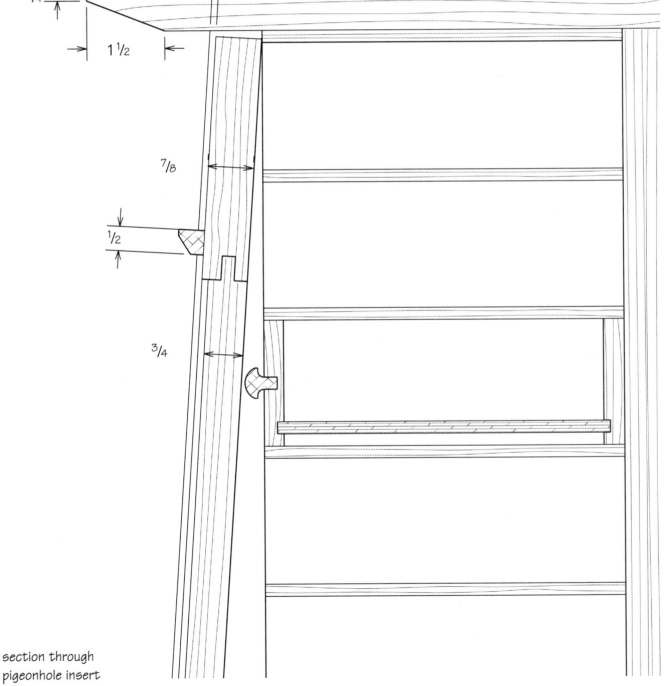

$^{1}/_{8}$

$^{1}/_{4}$

$1^{1}/_{2}$

$^{7}/_{8}$

$^{1}/_{2}$

$^{3}/_{4}$

section through
pigeonhole insert

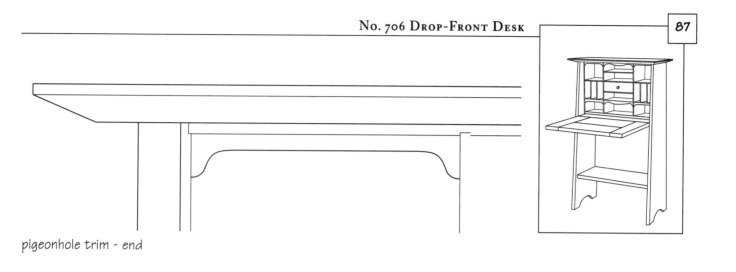

pigeonhole trim - end

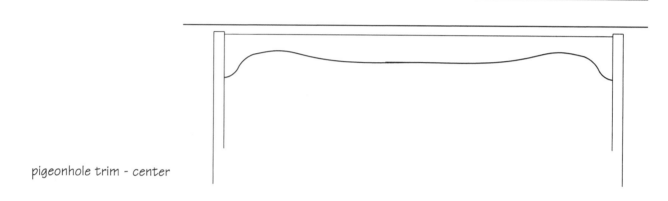

pigeonhole trim - center

Gustav Stickley No. 706 Drop-Front Desk

QTY	PART	SIZE	NOTES
2	Sides	$1 \times 11^{1}/_{8} \times 43^{1}/_{8}$	
1	Top	$^{7}/_{8} \times 11 \times 30$	
1	Lower Shelf	$^{3}/_{4} \times 9^{13}/_{16} \times 23^{3}/_{4}$	23 exposed between sides
1	Drop Front	$^{7}/_{8} \times 23 \times 21^{3}/_{8}$	Width of opening—trim for desired gaps—parts detailed below
2	Stiles	$^{7}/_{8} \times 3 \times 21^{3}/_{8}$	
1	Top Rail	$^{7}/_{8} \times 5 \times 18$	17 exposed
1	Bottom Rail	$^{7}/_{8} \times 3^{3}/_{8} \times 18$	17 exposed
1	Panel	$^{3}/_{4} \times 18 \times 14$	17 x 14 exposed
1	Applied Trim	$^{1}/_{2} \times ^{1}/_{2} \times 18$	
1	Back	$^{3}/_{4} \times 23^{3}/_{4} \times 33^{3}/_{8}$	23 exposed between sides— 33 exposed between top & shelf parts for "shiplap" back listed below
5	Back Planks	$^{3}/_{4} \times 5^{3}/_{16} \times 33^{3}/_{8}$	$^{3}/_{8}$ rabbets as detailed will yield back $23^{11}/_{16}$ wide planks should be NO wider, narrower if humid
	Pigeonhole Insert		
2	Outer uprights	$^{1}/_{4} \times 7^{3}/_{4} \times 14^{3}/_{4}$	
1	Bottom	$^{1}/_{2} \times 7^{3}/_{4} \times 22^{3}/_{4}$	$22^{1}/_{2}$ exposed between outer uprights
3	Top & shelves	$^{1}/_{4} \times 7^{3}/_{4} \times 22^{3}/_{4}$	$22^{1}/_{2}$ exposed between outer uprights
2	Upper Vert. Dividers	$^{1}/_{4} \times 7^{3}/_{4} \times 5^{5}/_{8}$	$5^{1}/_{2}$ exposed between top & shelf
6	Mid. Vert. Dividers	$^{1}/_{4} \times 7^{3}/_{4} \times 5^{9}/_{16}$	$5^{7}/_{16}$ exposed between shelves
2	Lower Vert. Dividers	$^{1}/_{4} \times 7^{3}/_{4} \times 2^{3}/_{4}$	$2^{5}/_{8}$ exposed between bottom & shelf
3	Horizontal Dividers	$^{1}/_{4} \times 7^{3}/_{4} \times 9^{3}/_{8}$	$9^{1}/_{4}$ exposed between vertical dividers
4	End Trim	$^{1}/_{4} \times 1 \times 6^{3}/_{8}$	
2	Middle Trim	$^{1}/_{4} \times 1 \times 9^{1}/_{4}$	

Gustav Stickley

NO. 708 DESK
WITH TWO DRAWERS
36" high x 40" wide x 22" deep

People don't write letters with pen and paper any more, probably because they don't have a terrific desk like this one. It would also make a good home for a laptop computer—good design is timeless.

Gustav Stickley No. 708 Desk with Two Drawers

QTY	PART	SIZE	NOTES
1	Top	1 x 22 x 40	
4	Legs	$1^3/_4$ x $1^3/_4$ x 29	
2	Side Panels	$3/_4$ x $18^1/_2$ x $14^1/_2$	parts detailed below—$17^1/_2$ exposed between legs
4	Stiles	$3/_4$ x $2^1/_2$ x $10^3/_8$	2 x $9^3/_8$ exposed
2	Top Rails	$3/_4$ x $2^1/_4$ x $18^1/_2$	$17^1/_2$ exposed
2	Bot. Rails	$3/_4$ x $2^7/_8$ x $18^1/_2$	$17^1/_2$ exposed
2	Panels	$1/_4$ x $14^1/_2$ x $10^3/_8$	$13^1/_2$ x $9^3/_8$ exposed
1	Back Panel	$3/_4$ x $34^1/_2$ x $14^1/_2$	parts detailed below—$33^1/_2$ exposed between legs
2	End Stiles	$3/_4$ x $2^1/_2$ x $10^3/_8$	2 x $9^3/_8$ exposed
1	Mid. Stile	$3/_4$ x 2 x $10^3/_8$	$9^3/_8$ exposed
1	Top Rail	$3/_4$ x $2^1/_4$ x $34^1/_2$	$33^1/_2$ exposed between legs
1	Bot. Rail	$3/_4$ x $2^7/_8$ x $34^1/_2$	$33^1/_2$ exposed between legs
2	Panels	$1/_4$ x $14^3/_4$ x $10^3/_8$	$13^1/_2$ x $9^3/_8$ exposed
1	Shelf	$3/_4$ x 10 x $34^1/_2$	34 exposed between side panels
1	Rail Below Drawers	$3/_4$ x $3^3/_4$ x $34^1/_2$	33 exposed between side panels
1	Drawer Divider	$3/_4$ x $4^3/_8$ x $19^5/_8$	$19^1/_4$ exposed
2	Drawer Fronts	$3/_4$ x $4^3/_8$ x $16^3/_8$	opening size—trim for desired gaps
	Letter Rack		
1	Back	$1/_2$ x 6 x 36	add to length for joints if desired
2	Outer Ends	$1/_2$ x 5 x 6	cut out radius
2	Inner Ends	$1/_2$ x $4^1/_2$ x 6	add to width for joints if desired—cut out radius
2	Mid. Dividers	$3/_8$ x $2^3/_4$ x $11^5/_8$	add to length for joints if desired
2	Fronts	$3/_8$ x $2^3/_8$ x $11^5/_8$	add to length for joints if desired
2	Bottoms	$1/_2$ x $4^1/_2$ x $11^5/_8$	4 exposed

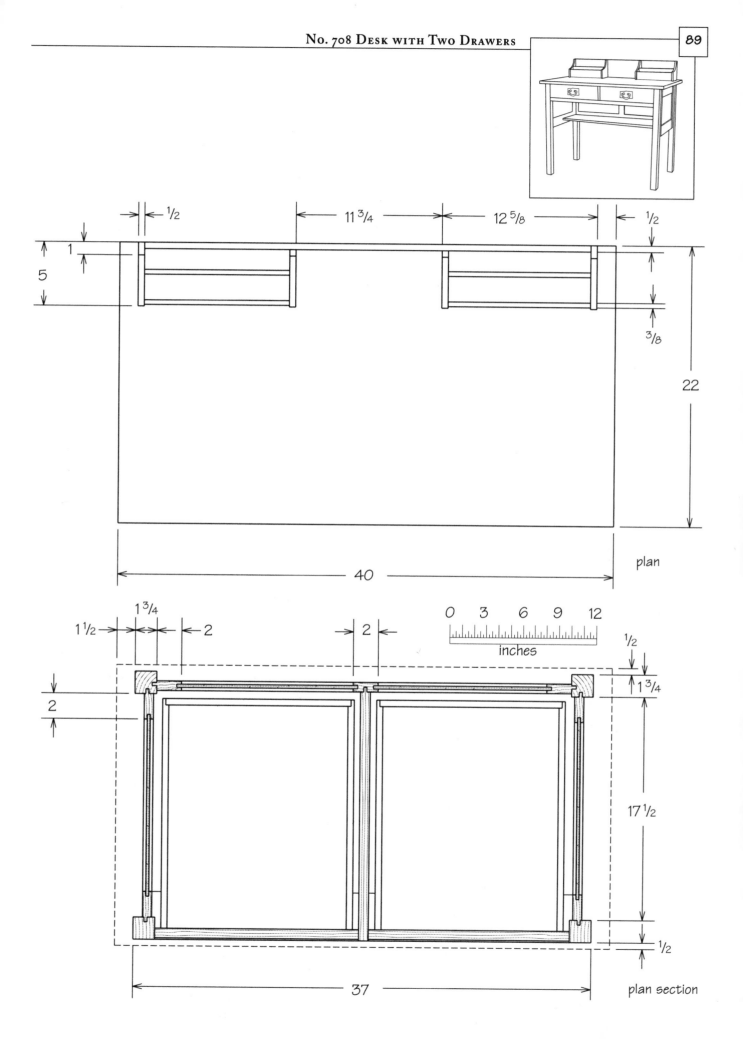

½   11 ¾   12 ⅝   ½

1

5

⅜

22

40

plan

1 ¾

1 ½   2   2   ½

0 3 6 9 12

inches

½

1 ¾

2

17 ½

½

37

plan section

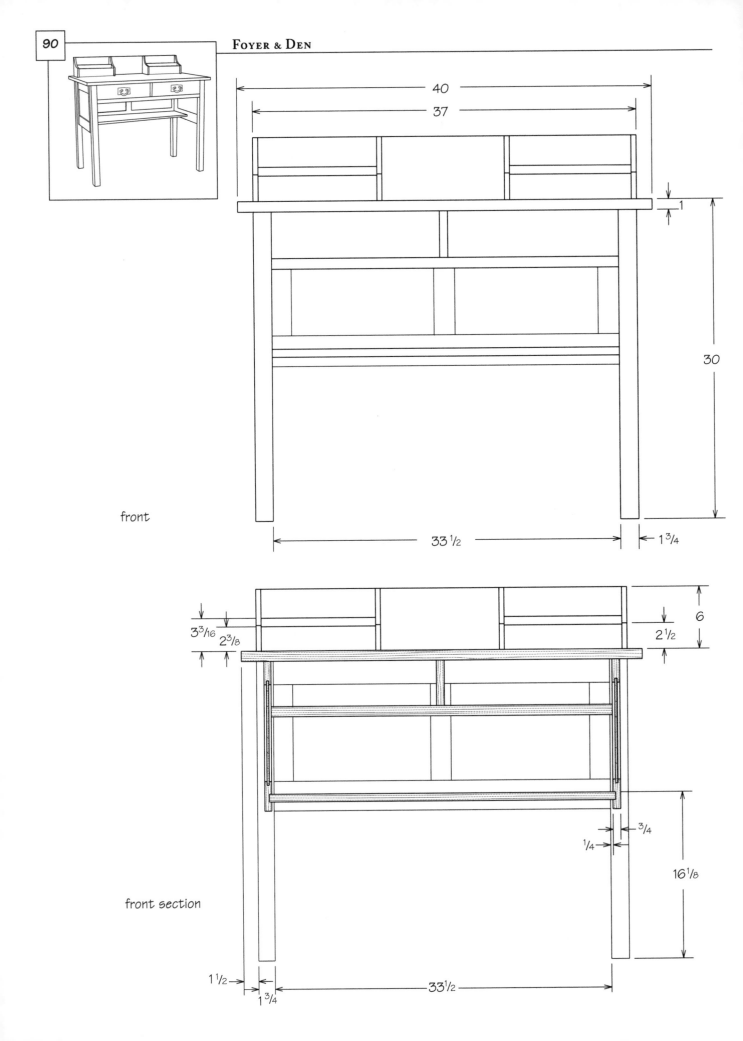

front

40

37

1

30

33 1/2

1 3/4

front section

3 3/16

2 3/8

6

2 1/2

3/4

1/4

16 1/8

1 1/2

1 3/4

33 1/2

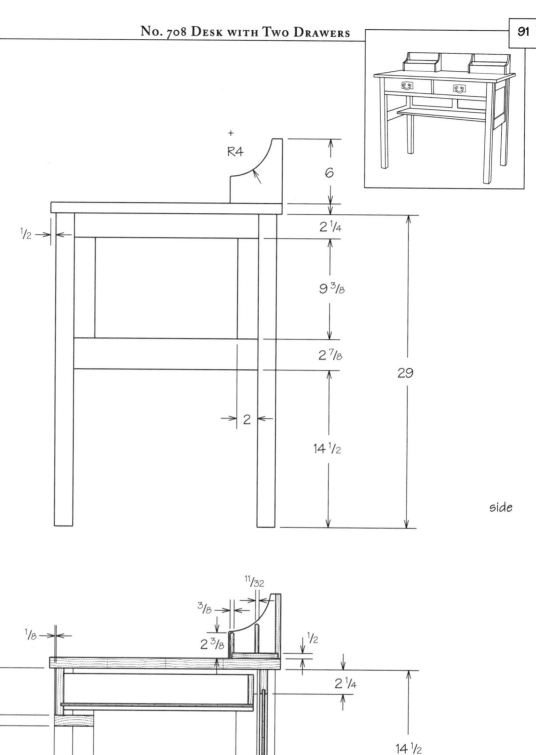

+
R4

6

1/2

2 1/4

9 3/8

2 7/8

2

14 1/2

29

side

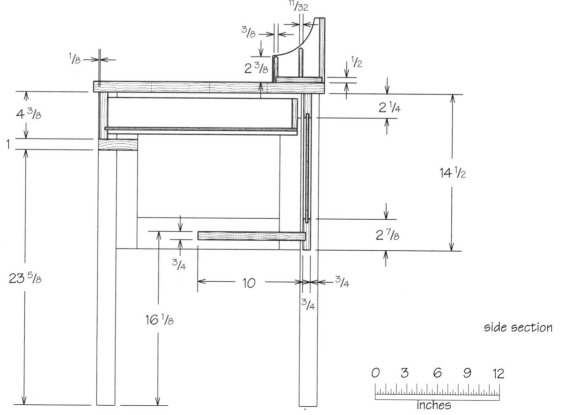

11/32

3/8

1/8

2 3/8

1/2

4 3/8

2 1/4

1

14 1/2

2 7/8

23 5/8

3/4

10

3/4

3/4

16 1/8

side section

0   3   6   9   12

inches

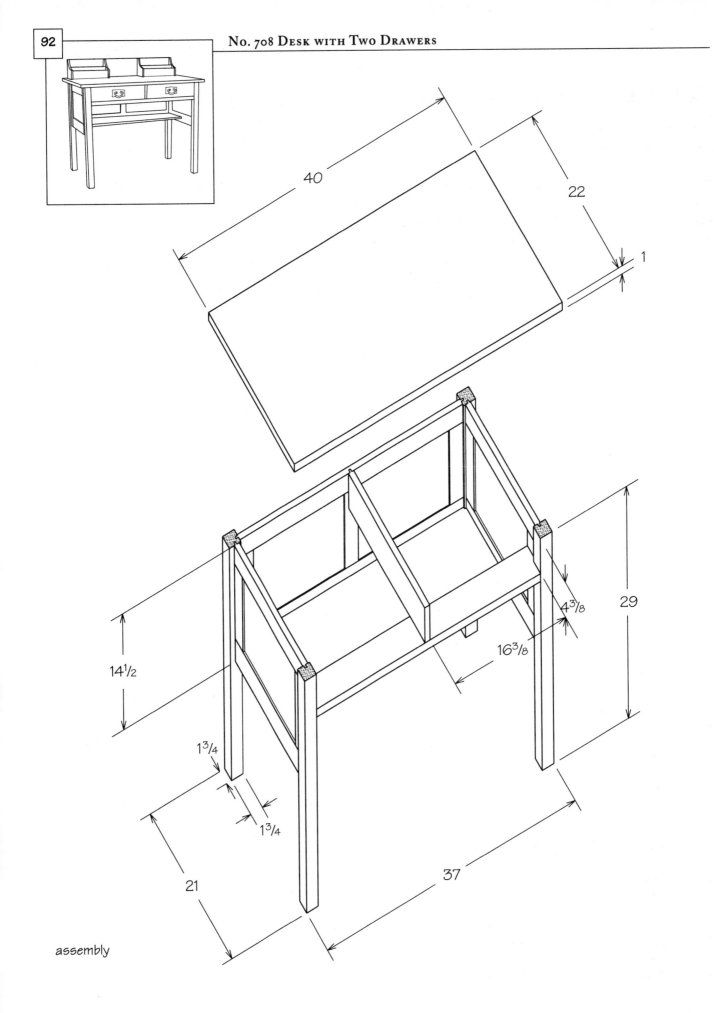

40

22

1

29

14¹/₂

4³/₈

16³/₈

1³/₄

1³/₄

21

37

assembly

ROYCROFT "LITTLE JOURNEYS" BOOK STAND

26" high x 26" wide x 14" deep

Produced after Elbert Hubbard's death to hold the complete set of his "Little Journeys" books, this piece was shipped knocked down from the Aurora, N.Y., giftshop. Four screws through table irons attach the top. Existing antiques are often a little wobbly, probably due to having been assembled by the customer. A ³/₄" x ³/₄" cleat along the inside of the legs at the top would be a structural improvement.

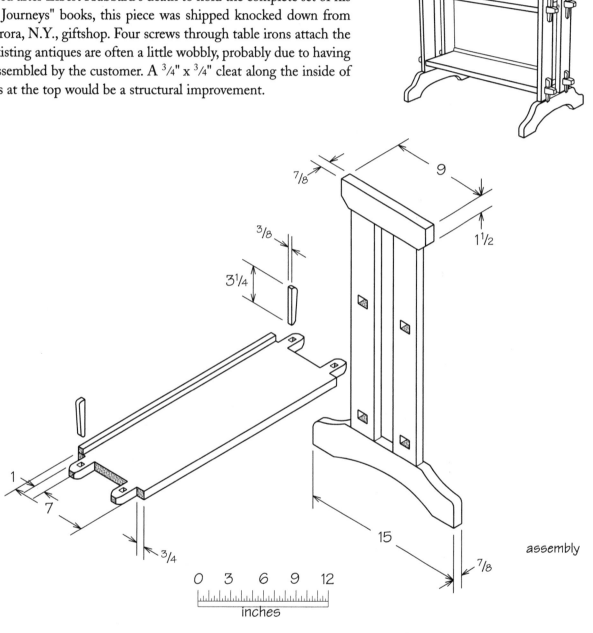

assembly

inches

	Roycroft "Little Journeys" Stand		
QTY	PART	SIZE	NOTES
1	Top	¹³/₁₆ x 14 x 26	
2	Feet	⁷/₈ x 3¹/₂ x 15	
2	Side Top Rails	³/₄ x 2¹/₄ x 9	
4	Legs	³/₄ x 2¹/₂ x 20¹⁵/₁₆	19⁷/₁₆ between tenon shoulders
2	Shelves	³/₄ x 7 x 25¹/₄	20³/₈ between tenon shoulders
2	Shelf Backs	¹/₂ x ¹/₂ x 20³/₈	
4	Keys	³/₈ x ⁷/₈ x 3¹/₄	

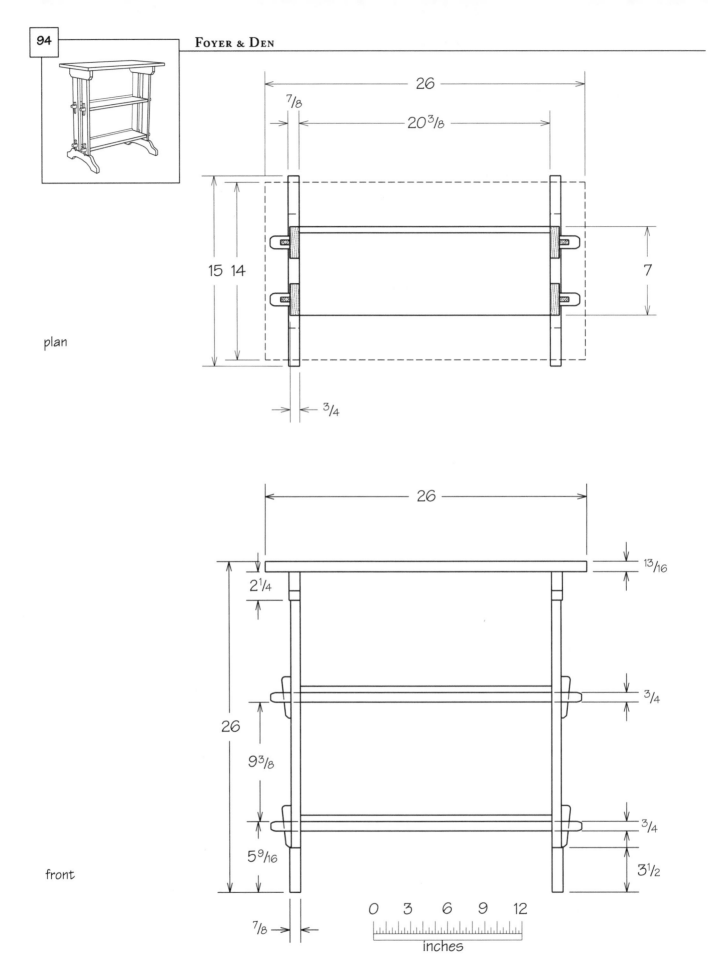

plan

front

26

20³/₈

7/8

15   14

7

3/4

26

2¹/₄

13/16

3/4

26

9³/₈

3/4

5⁹/₁₆

3¹/₂

7/8

0   3   6   9   12

inches

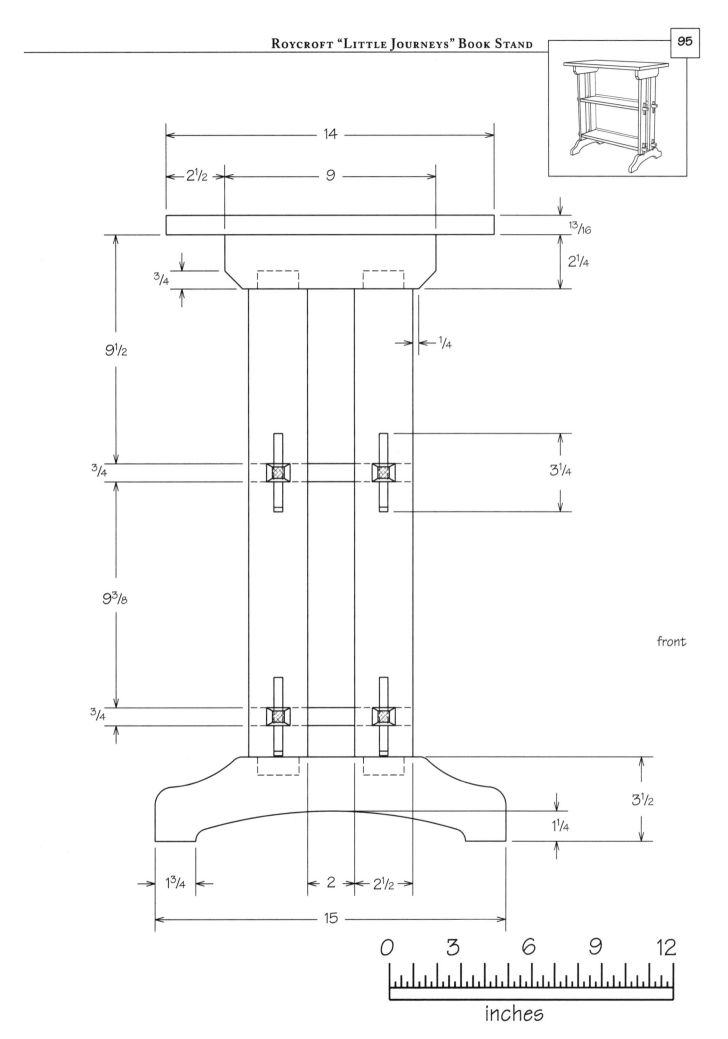

front

inches

BEDROOM

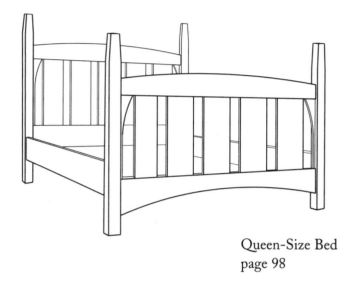

Queen-Size Bed
page 98

No. 641 Nightstand
page 101

No. 112 Wardrobe
page 104

No. 913 Bureau
page 110

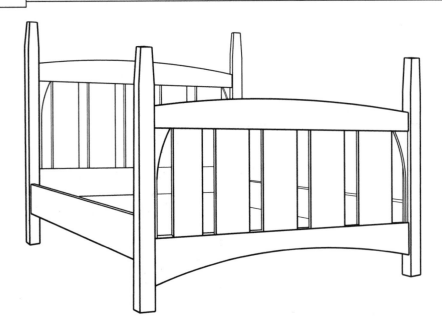

Gustav Stickley

QUEEN-SIZE BED
Designed by Harvey Ellis

The original of this bed had inlays in the slats on the head and foot boards, and apparently never went into production. The size has been modified slightly to accommodate a modern queen-size mattress and box spring.

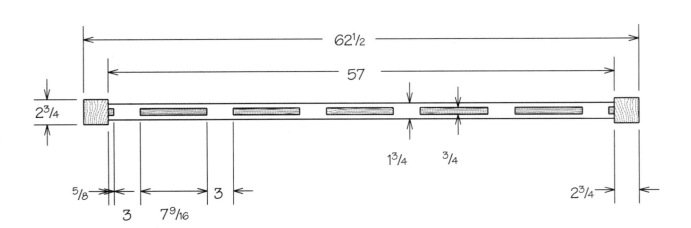

plan

	Gustav Stickley Queen-Size Bed		
QTY	PART	SIZE	NOTES
2	Headboard Legs	$2^3/_4$ x $2^3/_4$ x $56^1/_2$	
2	Footboard Legs	$2^3/_4$ x $2^3/_4$ x $44^7/_8$	
2	Top Rails	$1^3/_4$ x $6^1/_2$ x 60	57 between tenon shoulders
1	Headboard Bot. Rail	$1^3/_4$ x $7^1/_2$ x 60	57 between tenon shoulders
1	Footboard Bot. Rail	$1^3/_4$ x $8^1/_{16}$ x 60	57 between tenon shoulders
2	Headboard Corbels	$^3/_4$ x 3 x $22^5/_{16}$	cut to curve
2	Footboard Corbels	$^3/_4$ x 3 x $18^3/_{16}$	cut to curve
5	Headboard Slats	$^3/_4$ x $7^9/_{16}$ x $24^{13}/_{16}$	$22^5/_{16}$ between tenon shoulders
5	Footboard Slats	$^3/_4$ x $7^9/_{16}$ x $19^{11}/_{16}$	$18^3/_{16}$ between tenon shoulders
2	Bed Rails	1 x $7^1/_2$ x 80*	*double check length with mattress
2	Bed Slat Supports	1 x 1 x 80*	*double check length with mattress

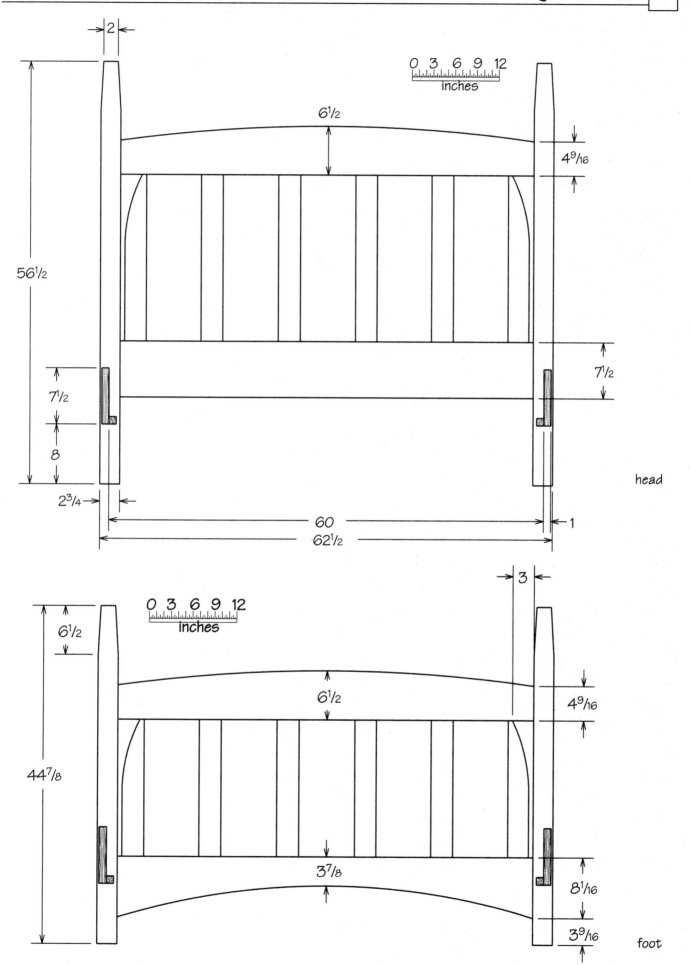

2

0 3 6 9 12
inches

6½

4⁹⁄₁₆

56½

7½

7½

8

head

2³⁄₄

60

62½

1

3

6½

0 3 6 9 12
inches

6½

4⁹⁄₁₆

44⁷⁄₈

3⁷⁄₈

8¹⁄₁₆

3⁹⁄₁₆

foot

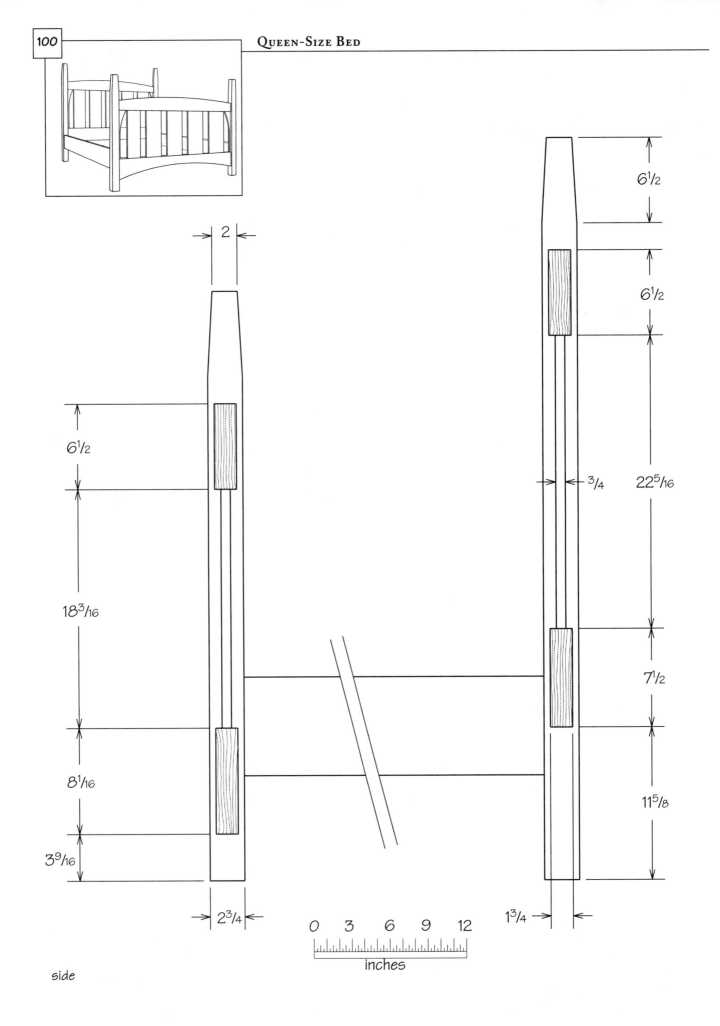

side

Gustav Stickley

No. 641 Nightstand
29" high x 20" wide x 18" deep

This simple little stand will work very well with the Ellis bed and No. 913 bureau (page 110). The nightstand could also be used as an end-table, with or without its backsplash.

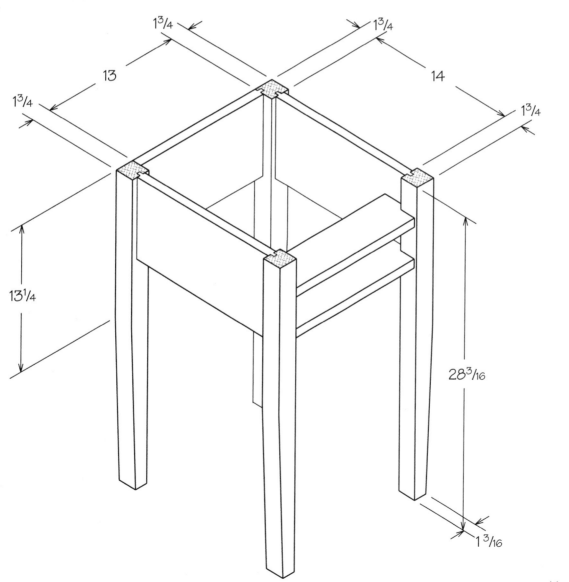

assembly

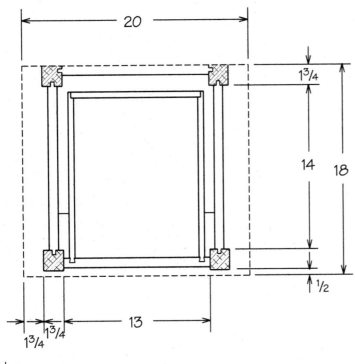

plan

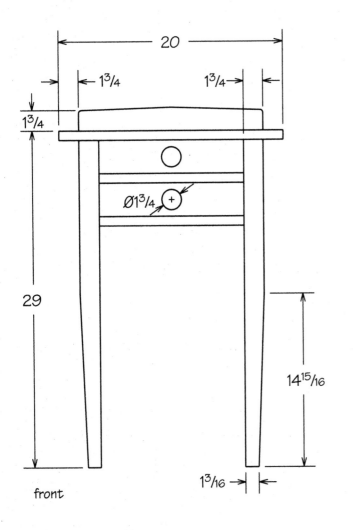

front

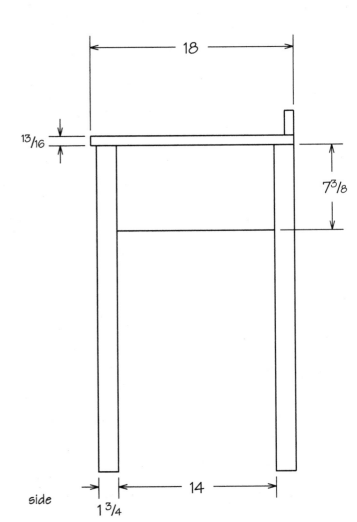

side

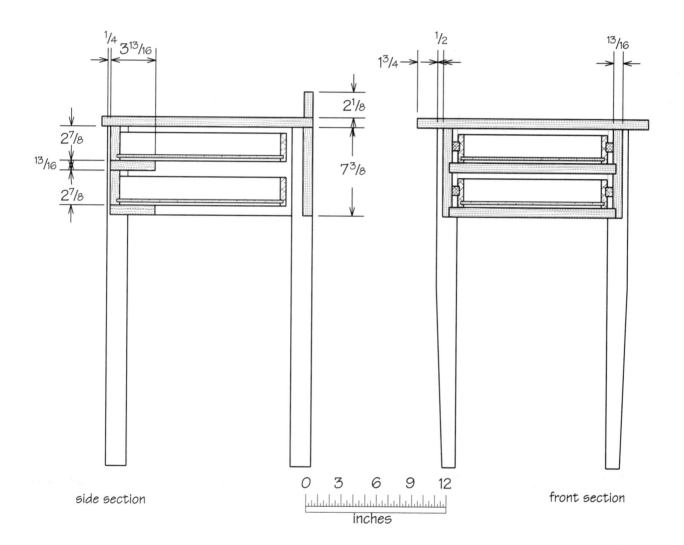

side section

0   3   6   9   12
inches

front section

Gustav Stickley No. 641 Nightstand

QTY	PART	SIZE	NOTES
1	Top	$^{13}/_{16}$ x 18 x 20	
4	Legs	$1^3/_4$ x $1^3/_4$ x $28^3/_{16}$	
2	Sides	$^{13}/_{16}$ x $7^3/_8$ x 15	14 between tenon shoulders
1	Back	$^{13}/_{16}$ x $7^3/_8$ x 14	13 between tenon shoulders
2	Rails	$^{13}/_{16}$ x $3^{13}/_{16}$ x $13^7/_8$	biscuit or pocket screw to sides or add for tenons
2	Drawer Fronts	$^{13}/_{16}$ x $2^7/_8$ x 13	opening size—trim for desired gaps
1	Backsplash	$^{13}/_{16}$ x $2^1/_8$ x $16^1/_2$	

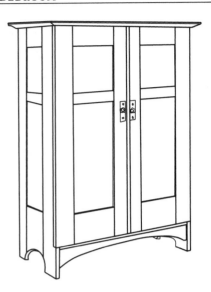

L. & J. G. Stickley

NO. 112 WARDROBE
60" high x 50" wide x 22½" deep

The hanger slide-out on the right side could be replaced with a rod going from side to side, although there is barely enough room to do so. Because of the width of this cabinet, and the weight of all the drawers, it wouldn't be a bad idea to put in a support in the middle of the bottom, running to the floor. Also note that the door overlays the front of the case and is notched into the sides.

L. & J.G. Stickley No. 112 Wardrobe

QTY	PART	SIZE	NOTES
1	Top	1 x 22½ x 50	
2	Side Panels	¾ x 21⁵⁄₁₆ x 59	parts detailed below
4	Stiles	¾ x 5⅝ x 59	front stiles notched @ door
2	Top Rails	¾ x 4¾ x 11¹⁄₁₆	10¹⁄₁₆ between tongues
2	Mid Rails	¾ x 2⅝ x 11¹⁄₁₆	10¹⁄₁₆ between tongues
2	Bot. Rails	¾ x 12¹⁄₁₆ x 11¹⁄₁₆	10¹⁄₁₆ between tongues
2	Upper Side Panels	¼ x 11¹⁄₁₆ x 12¼	10¹⁄₁₆ x 11¼ exposed
2	Lower Side Panels	¼ x 11¹⁄₁₆ x 27³⁄₁₆	10¹⁄₁₆ x 26³⁄₁₆ exposed
1	Back Panel	¾ x 46⁷⁄₈ x 52⅛	46⅛ x 52¾ exposed—parts detailed below
2	Outer Stiles	¾ x 4 x 52⅛	
2	Top & Bottom Rails	¾ x 4 x 39⅞	38⅞ between tongues
1	Middle Stile	¾ x 4 x 45⅛	44⅛ between tongues
2	Middle Rails	¾ x 4 x 17⁷⁄₁₆	16⁷⁄₁₆ between tongues
4	Panels	¼ x 17⁷⁄₁₆ x 21¹⁄₁₆	16⁷⁄₁₆ x 20¹⁄₁₆ exposed
1	Bottom	¾ x 21⁵⁄₁₆ x 46⅛	
1	Vertical Divider	¾ x 20⁹⁄₁₆ x 51¾	
2	Uprights	¾ x 4 x 51¾	
1	Door Divider	¾ x 1⅛ x 51¾	
6	Hor. Div. Bet. Dwrs.	¾ x 19¹³⁄₁₆ x 22⁵⁄₁₆	biscuit or pocket screw to side
1	Ver. Div. Bet. Dwrs	¾ x 3¾ x 19¹³⁄₁₆	
2	Drawer Fronts	¾ x 3¾ x 10²⁵⁄₃₂	opening size—trim for desired gaps
5	Drawer Fronts	¾ x 5⅜ x 22⁵⁄₁₆	opening size—trim for desired gaps
2	Doors	¾ x 23¼ x 51¾	parts detailed below—opening size trim for desired gaps
2	Hinge Stiles	¾ x 6 x 51¾	
2	Inner Stiles	¾ x 4¼ x 51¾	
2	Top Rails	¾ x 4¾ x 14	13 between tongues
2	Middle Rails	¾ x 2⅝ x 14	13 between tongues
2	Bottom Rails	¾ x 7⅜ x 14	13 between tongues
2	Top Panels	¼ x 14 x 12¼	13 x 11¼ exposed
2	Bottom Panels	¼ x 14 x 26¾	13 x 25¾ exposed
2	Arched Aprons	¾ x 4 x 46⅛	add to length for joint or use biscuits or pocket screws
2	Bottom Cleats	¾ x 1½ x 19⁹⁄₁₆	
1	Hanger Slide		parts detailed below
1	Front	¾ x 4 x 6	
2	Cleats @ Top	¾ x 1¼ x 17½	
1	Slide	¾ x 5 x 17½	
1	Back	¾ x 3¼ x 6	
1	Rod	1 diameter x 19	

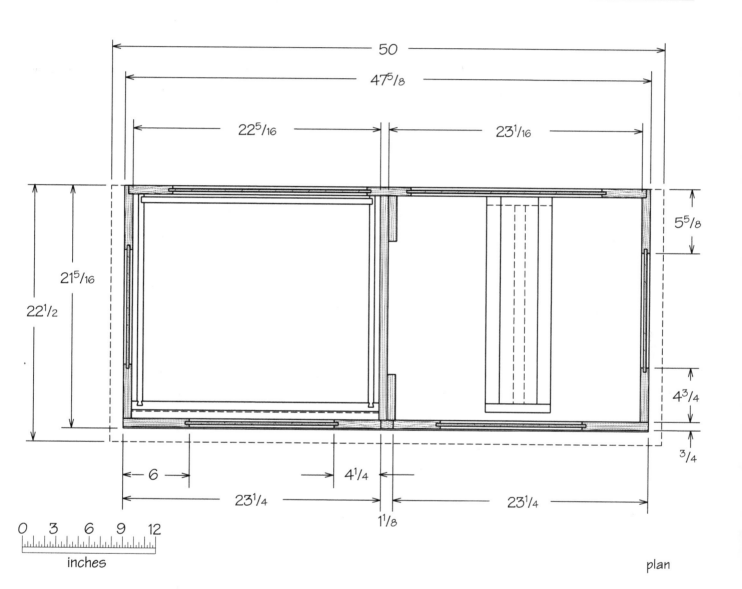

50

47⁵/₈

22⁵/₁₆

23¹/₁₆

5⁵/₈

21⁵/₁₆

22¹/₂

4³/₄

³/₄

6

4¹/₄

23¹/₄

23¹/₄

1¹/₈

0 3 6 9 12

inches

plan

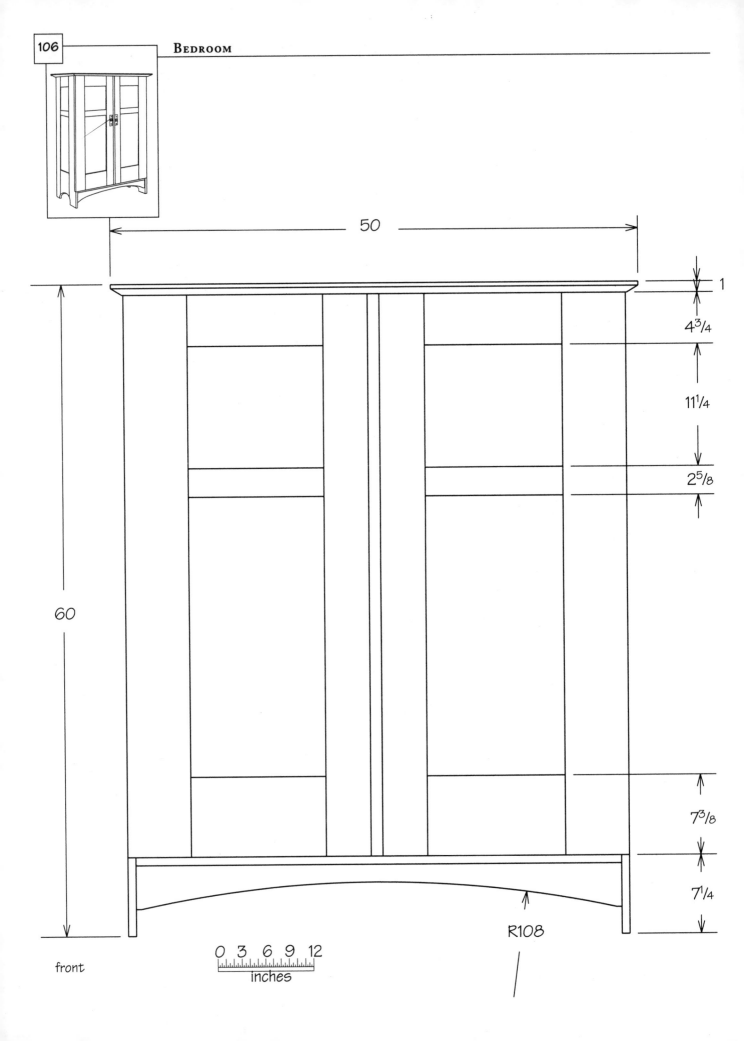

50

1

4³/₄

11¹/₄

2⁵/₈

60

7³/₈

7¹/₄

R108

front

0 3 6 9 12
inches

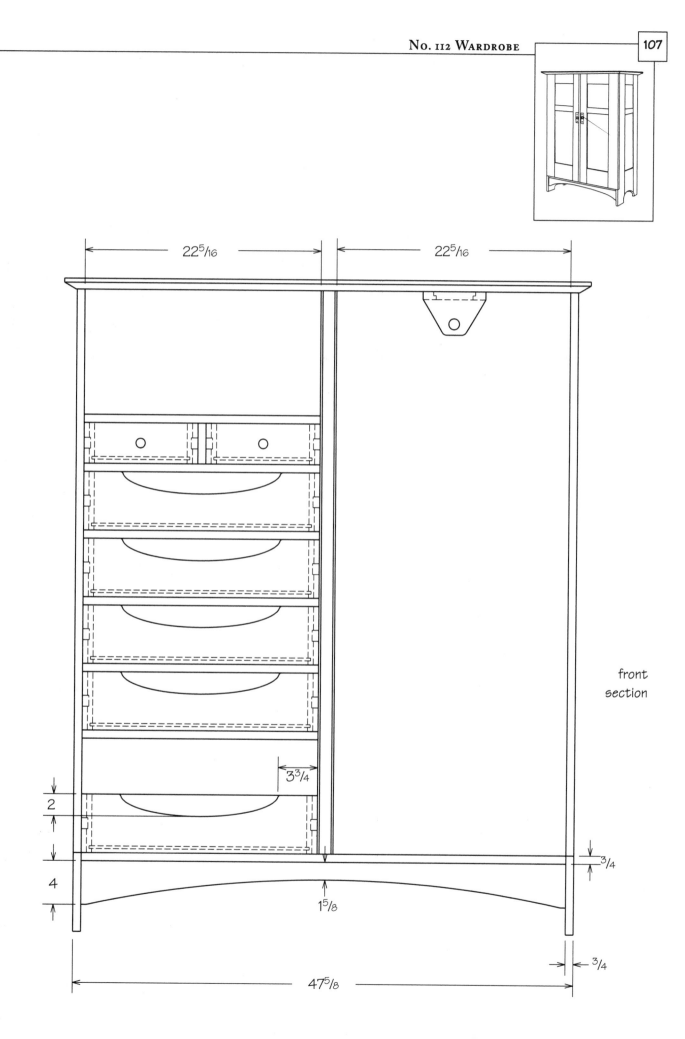

22⁵/₁₆

22⁵/₁₆

front
section

3³/₄

2

3/4

4

1⁵/₈

3/4

47⁵/₈

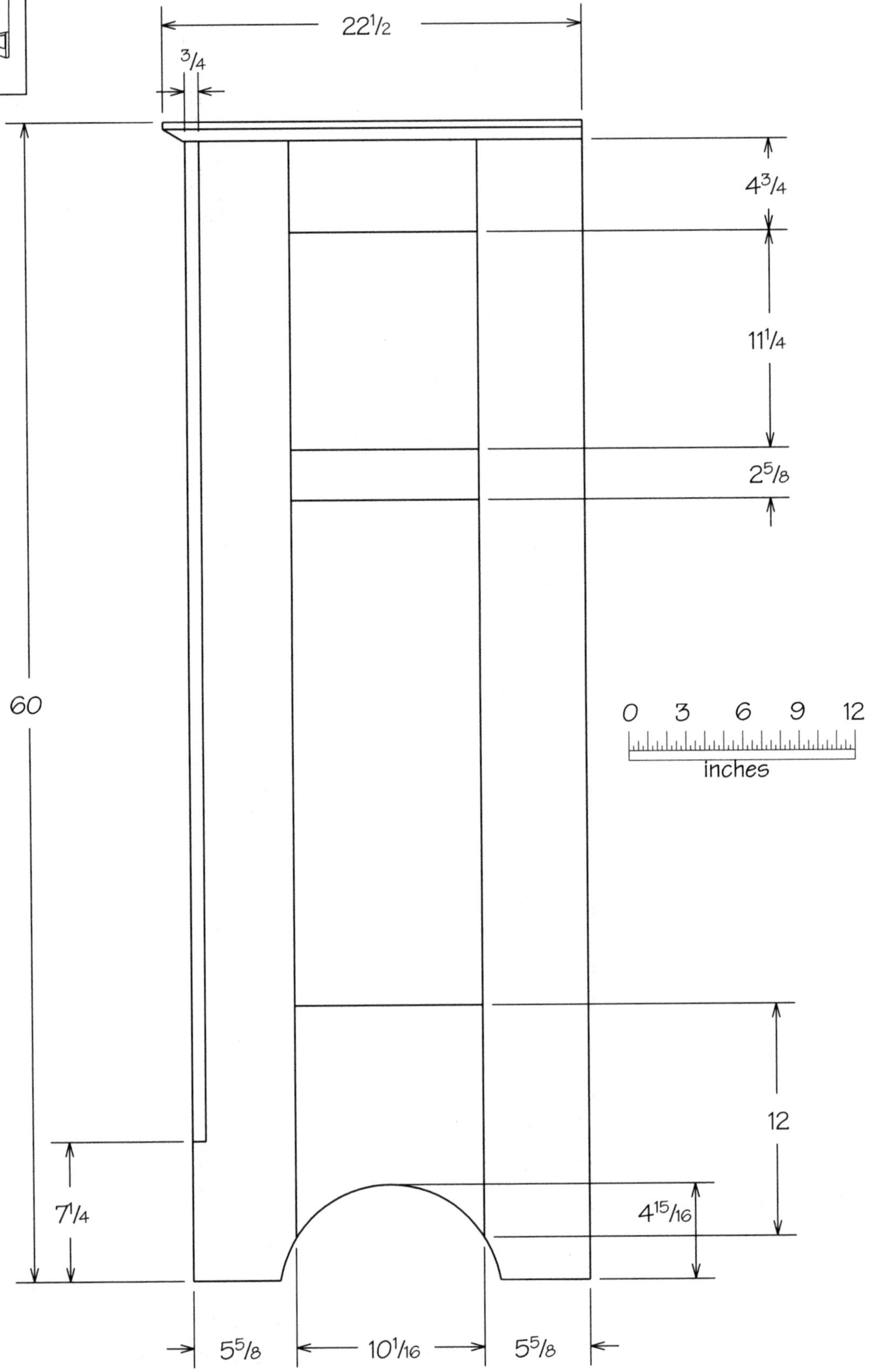

3/4

22 1/2

4 3/4

11 1/4

2 5/8

60

0   3   6   9   12

inches

12

4 15/16

7 1/4

side

5 5/8   10 1/16   5 5/8

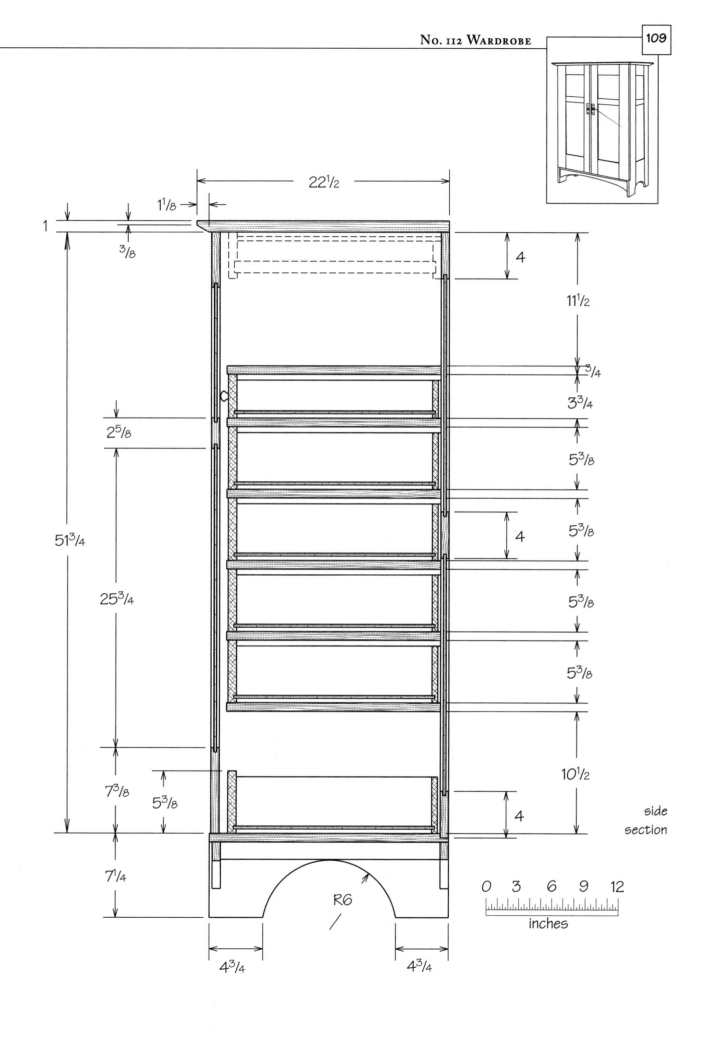

22½

1⅛

1

⅜

4

11½

³/4

3³/4

5³/8

4

5³/8

5³/8

51³/4

2⁵/8

25³/4

5³/8

10½

7³/8

5³/8

4

7¼

R6

side
section

4³/4

4³/4

0   3   6   9   12

inches

Gustav Stickley

NO. 913 BUREAU

50" high x 36" wide x 20" deep

Designed by Harvey Ellis, this bureau and several related pieces are among the best-proportioned furniture ever manufactured. Small in stature, its dignified appearance and simple elegance make it seem much larger when viewed in isolation. This piece appeared in the old catalogs in several variations—different types of hardware, and with or without the paneled sides.

The legs have often been described as "bowed," but they are actually tapered toward the top as well as the bottom. In the front elevation there is a dimension indicating where the two lines meet.

Gustav Stickley No. 913 Bureau

QTY.	PART	SIZE	NOTES
1	Top	$^{13}/_{16}$ x 20 x 36	
1	Backsplash	$^{13}/_{16}$ x $2^{5}/_{8}$ x 32	
4	Legs	$1^{3}/_{4}$ x $2^{1}/_{8}$ x $49^{3}/_{16}$	
2	Side Panels	$^{13}/_{16}$ x 17 x $45^{3}/_{4}$	16 exposed between legs—parts detailed below
4	Side Stiles	$^{13}/_{16}$ x 5 x $45^{3}/_{4}$	$4^{1}/_{2}$ exposed
2	Side Top Rails	$^{13}/_{16}$ x $4^{3}/_{8}$ x 8	7 between tongues
2	Side Mid Rails	$^{13}/_{16}$ x $3^{1}/_{4}$ x 8	7 between tongues
2	Side Bot. Rails	$^{13}/_{16}$ x $4^{3}/_{4}$ x 8	7 between tongues
2	Side Upper Panels	$^{1}/_{4}$ x 8 x $8^{15}/_{16}$	7 x $7^{15}/_{16}$ exposed
2	Side Lower Panels	$^{1}/_{4}$ x 8 x $26^{3}/_{8}$	7 x $25^{3}/_{8}$ exposed
1	Back Panel	$^{13}/_{16}$ x $29^{1}/_{4}$ x $45^{3}/_{4}$	$28^{1}/_{4}$ exposed between legs-parts detailed below
2	Back Stiles	$^{13}/_{16}$ x 5 x $45^{3}/_{4}$	$4^{1}/_{2}$ exposed
1	Back Top Rail	$^{13}/_{16}$ x $4^{3}/_{8}$ x $20^{1}/_{4}$	$19^{1}/_{4}$ between tongues
1	Back Mid Rail	$^{13}/_{16}$ x $4^{1}/_{4}$ x $20^{1}/_{4}$	$19^{1}/_{4}$ between tongues
1	Back Bot. Rail	$^{13}/_{16}$ x $4^{3}/_{4}$ x $20^{1}/_{4}$	$19^{1}/_{4}$ between tongues
1	Back Upper Panel	$^{1}/_{4}$ x $20^{1}/_{4}$ x $18^{15}/_{32}$	$19^{1}/_{4}$ x $17^{15}/_{32}$ exposed
1	Back Llower Panel	$^{1}/_{4}$ x $20^{1}/_{4}$ x $15^{19}/_{32}$	$19^{1}/_{4}$ x $14^{19}/_{32}$ exposed
3	Rails Between Drawers	$^{13}/_{16}$ x $4^{1}/_{2}$ x $29^{1}/_{4}$	$28^{1}/_{4}$ between tenons
4	Rails Between Drawers	$^{13}/_{16}$ x $4^{1}/_{2}$ x $14^{15}/_{32}$	$13^{23}/_{32}$ between tenons
1	Vert. Div. Bet. Dwrs.	$^{13}/_{16}$ x $4^{1}/_{2}$ x $14^{3}/_{4}$	screw through rail below, or add to length for joint
1	Bottom Front Rail	$^{13}/_{16}$ x $3^{11}/_{16}$ x $29^{1}/_{4}$	$28^{1}/_{4}$ between tenons
1	Arched Ffront Apron	$^{13}/_{16}$ x $4^{3}/_{4}$ x $30^{1}/_{4}$	$28^{1}/_{4}$ between tenons
6	Drawer Fronts	$^{13}/_{16}$ x $4^{3}/_{8}$ x $13^{23}/_{32}$	opening size—trim for desired gaps
1	Drawer Front	$^{13}/_{16}$ x $6^{1}/_{4}$ x $28^{1}/_{4}$	opening size—trim for desired gaps
1	Drawer Front	$^{13}/_{16}$ x $9^{5}/_{16}$ x $28^{1}/_{4}$	opening size—trim for desired gaps
1	Drawer Fornt	$^{13}/_{16}$ x 8 x $28^{1}/_{4}$	opening size—trim for desired gaps

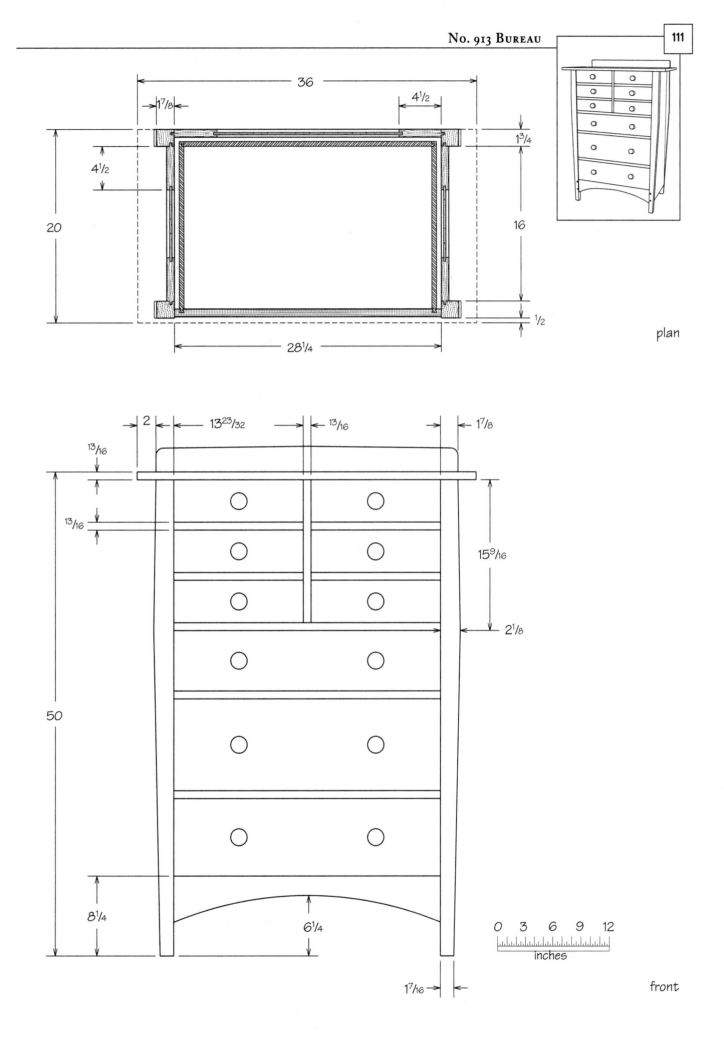

36

4¹/₂

1⁷/₈

20

4¹/₂

1³/₄

16

¹/₂

28¹/₄

plan

2

13²³/₃₂

13/₁₆

1⁷/₈

13/₁₆

13/₁₆

15⁹/₁₆

2¹/₈

50

8¹/₄

6¹/₄

1⁷/₁₆

0 3 6 9 12

inches

front

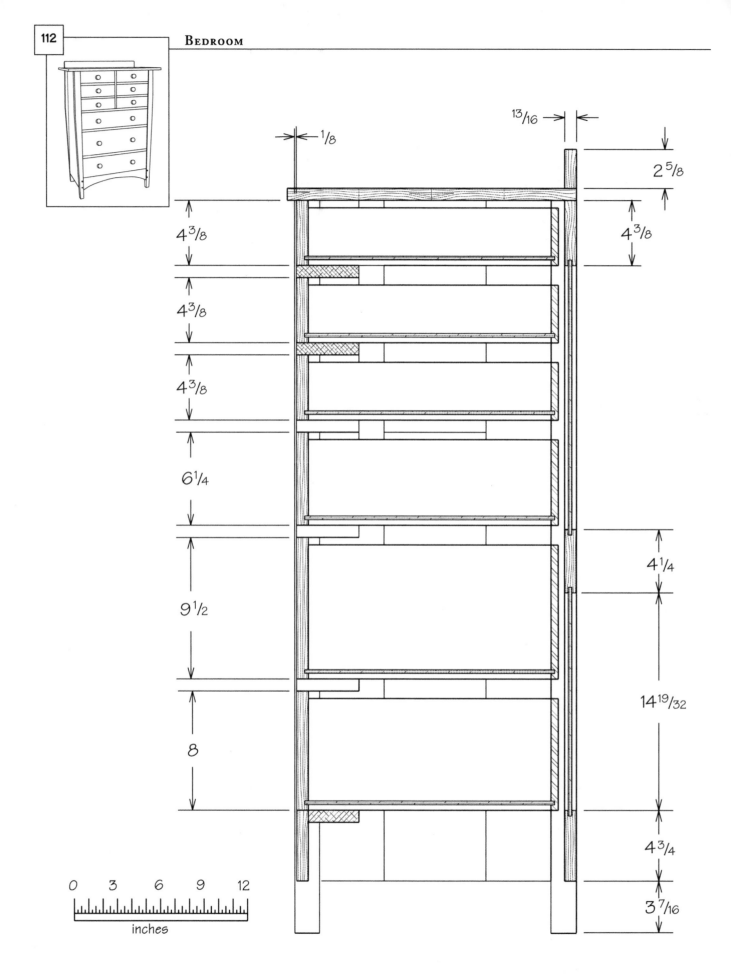

1/8

13/16

2 5/8

4 3/8

4 3/8

4 3/8

4 3/8

4 3/8

6 1/4

4 1/4

9 1/2

14 19/32

8

4 3/4

3 7/16

0   3   6   9   12

inches

side section

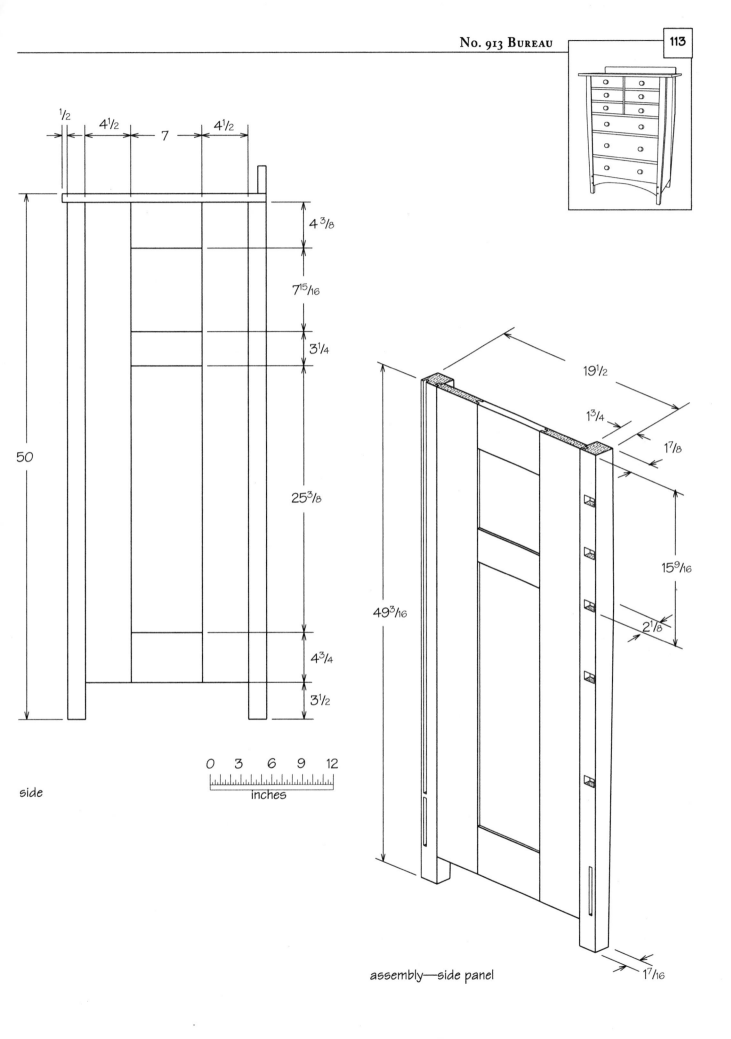

1/2   4 1/2   7   4 1/2

50

4 3/8

7 15/16

3 1/4

25 3/8

4 3/4

3 1/2

0   3   6   9   12
inches

side

19 1/2

1 3/4

1 7/8

15 9/16

2 1/8

49 3/16

1 7/16

assembly—side panel

Dining Room

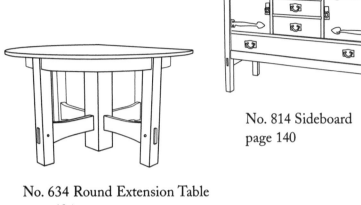

No. 814 Sideboard
page 140

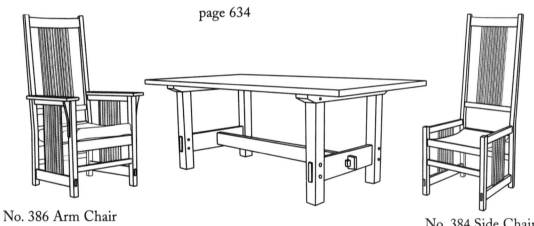

No. 634 Round Extension Table
page 634

No. 386 Arm Chair
page 129

No. 622 Trestle Table
page 116

No. 384 Side Chair
page 126

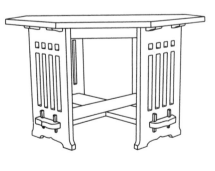

Limbert Octagonal Table
page 119

No. 815 China Cabinet
page 136

No. 802 Sideboard
page 132

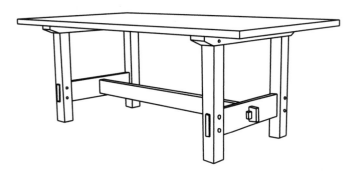

Gustav Stickley

NO. 622 TRESTLE TABLE

42" x 84" x 30"

A very substantial table, yet much lighter in appearance than the L. & J.G. Stickley No. 599 table. Fasten the top with large screws in elongated holes through the top stretcher. This table can be made to knock down for moving if you don't glue the joints at the keyed tenons.

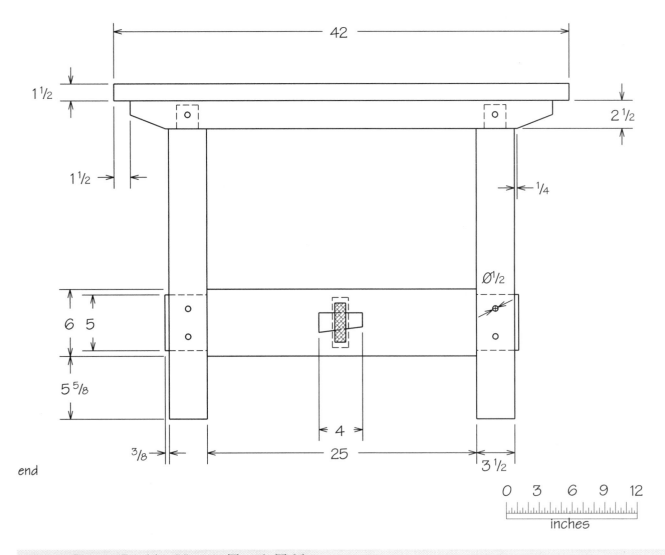

end

inches

Gustav Stickley No. 622 Trestle Table

QTY	PART	SIZE	NOTES
1	Top	$1\frac{1}{2}$ x 42 x 84	
4	Legs	$3\frac{1}{2}$ x $3\frac{1}{2}$ x 28	26 floor to tenon shoulder
2	Top Stretchers	$2\frac{1}{2}$ x $3\frac{1}{2}$ x 39	
2	Bottom Stretchers	$1\frac{3}{4}$ x 6 x $32\frac{3}{4}$	25 between tenon shoulders
1	Stretcher	$1\frac{1}{2}$ x $4\frac{1}{2}$ x $65\frac{1}{4}$	$54\frac{3}{4}$ between tenon shoulders
2	Keys	$\frac{3}{4}$ x $2\frac{3}{4}$ x 4	

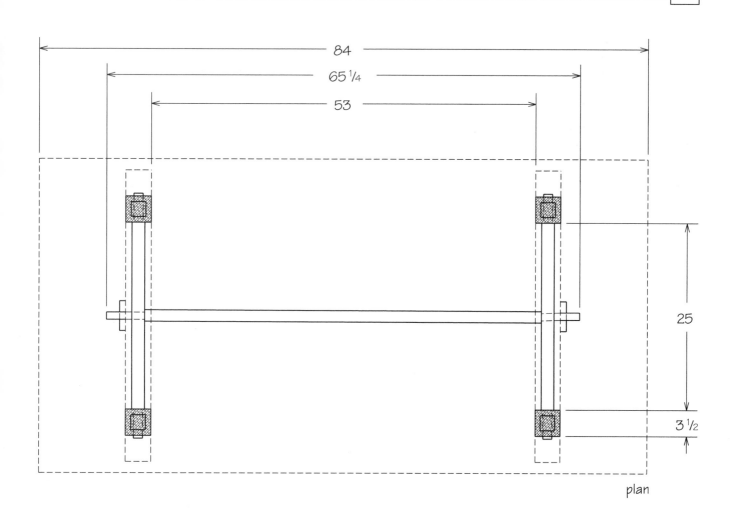

plan

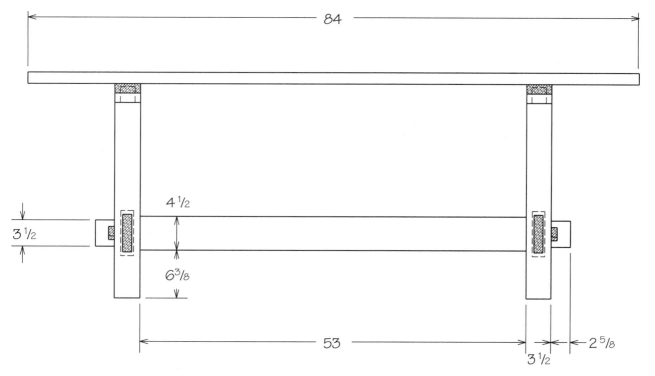

front

0 3 6 9 12
inches

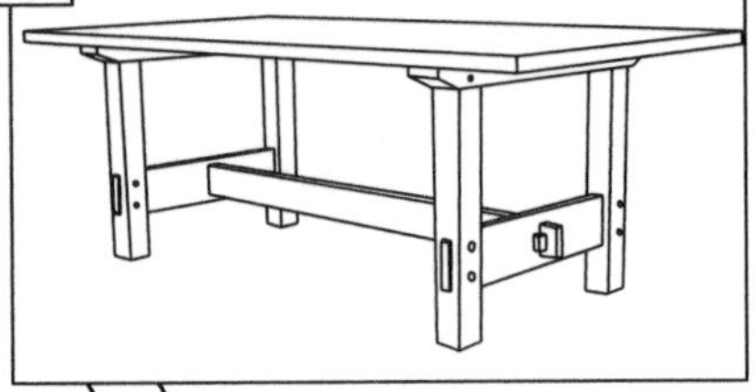

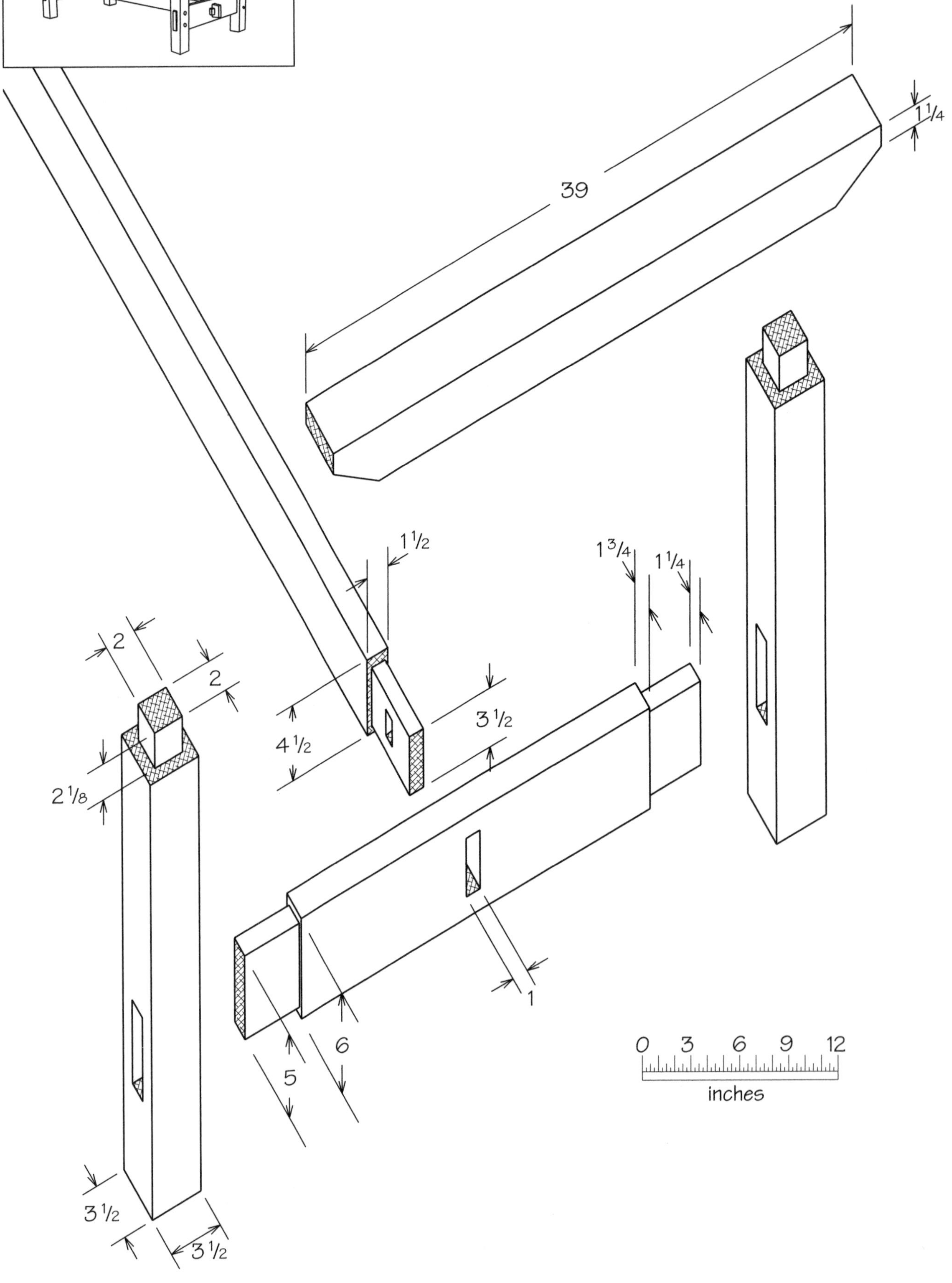

39

$1\frac{1}{4}$

$1\frac{1}{2}$

$1\frac{3}{4}$ $1\frac{1}{4}$

$3\frac{1}{2}$

$4\frac{1}{2}$

2   2

$2\frac{1}{8}$

1

6

5

$3\frac{1}{2}$

$3\frac{1}{2}$

0   3   6   9   12

inches

Charles Limbert

OCTAGONAL TABLE
48" x 48" x 29^1/$_2$" high

The corbels below the top are fake-screwed into the uprights. Make the upright pieces by ripping the stock, cutting out the openings, and gluing the pieces back together. Use dowels to keep everything aligned during the glue-up.

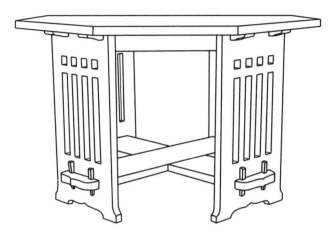

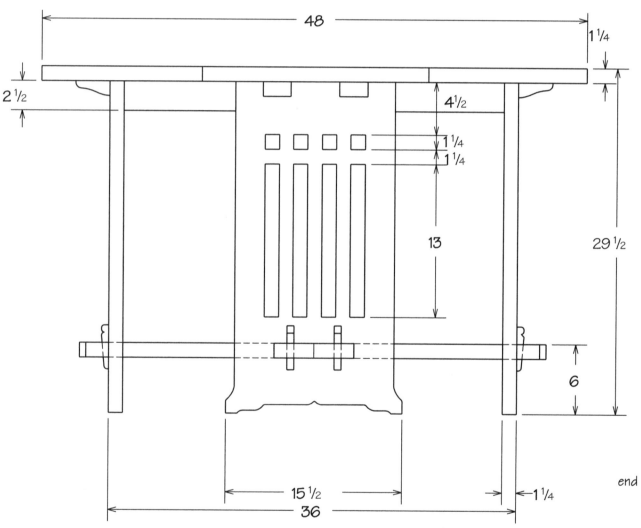

end

Limbert Octagonal Table

Qty	Part	Size	Notes
1	Top	1^1/$_4$ x 48 x 48	
4	Legs	1^1/$_4$ x 15^1/$_2$* x 28^1/$_4$	finished width—add 1^1/$_2$" for saw kerfs and planing
4	Top Stretchers	1^1/$_4$ x 2^1/$_2$ x 16^9/$_{32}$	
2	Bottom Stretchers	1^1/$_4$ x 8 x 41^1/$_8$	33^1/$_2$ between tenons—half lap together in middle
8	Keys	^{5}/$_8$ x ^{5}/$_8$ x 3^3/$_4$	
8	Top Corbels	1^1/$_4$ x 2^1/$_2$ x 3	

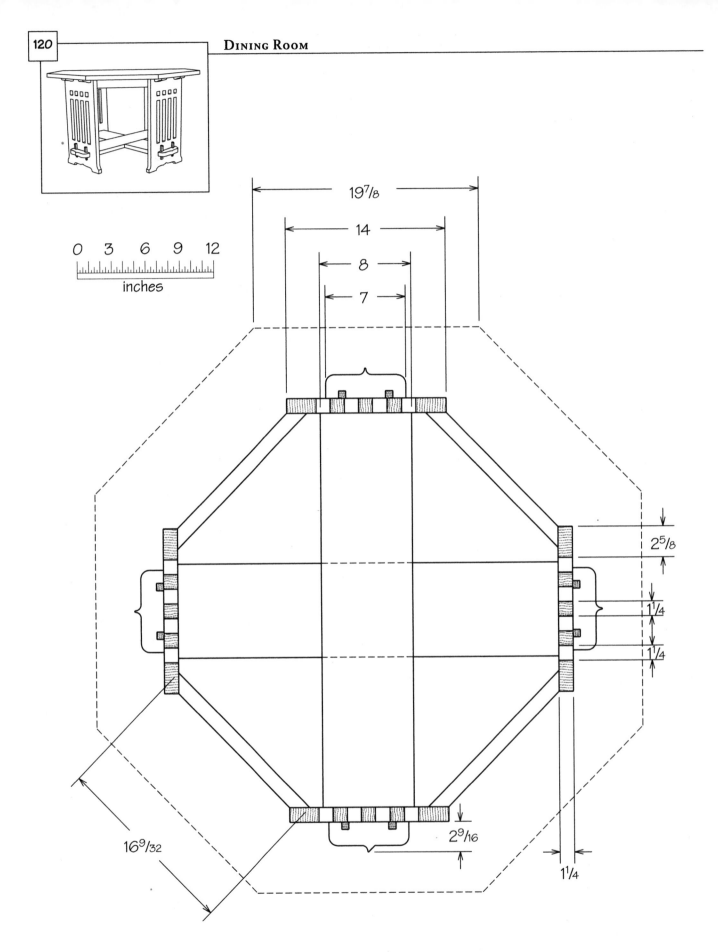

plan

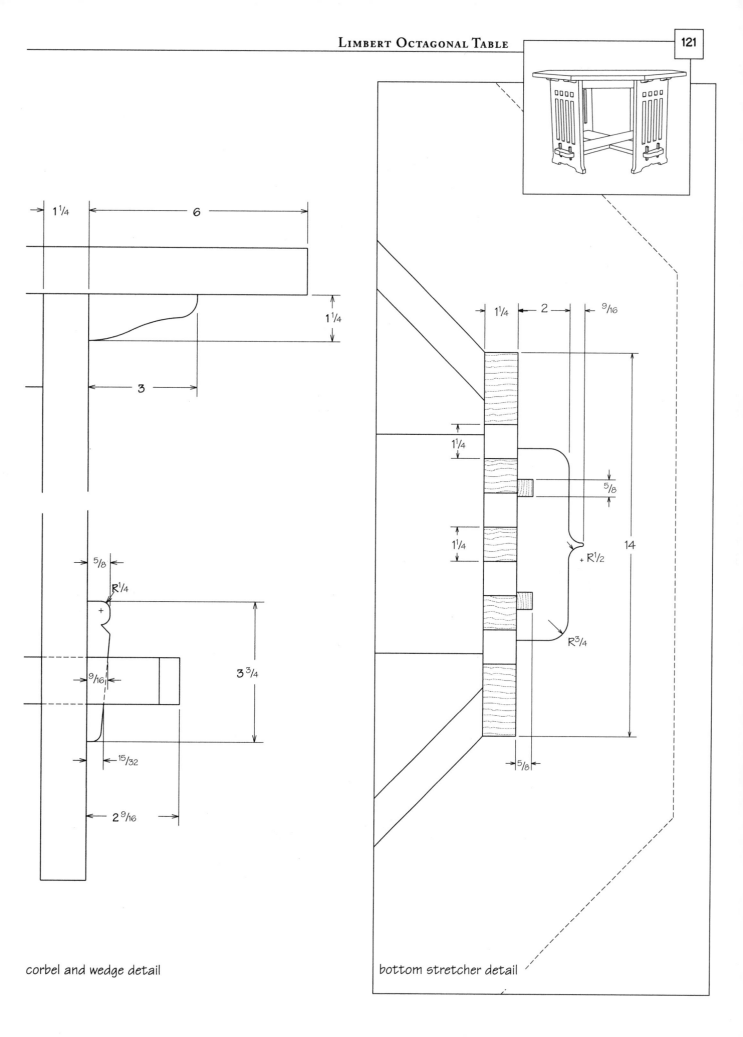

1¼

6

1¼

3

⁵/₈

R¼

+

⁹/₁₆

3 ³/₄

¹⁵/₃₂

2 ⁹/₁₆

corbel and wedge detail

1¼

2

⁹/₁₆

1¼

1¼

⁵/₈

14

+ R¹/₂

R³/₄

⁵/₈

bottom stretcher detail

Gustav Stickley

No. 634 Round Extension Table

54" x 29" high

This design has been attributed to LaMont Warner, Stickley's chief draftsman from 1900-1906. It is designed to extend, but can be made as a fixed table.

If made as an extension table, a wooden extension mechanism is bolted to a plate fixed to the tops of the two halves of the pedestal. Two dowels align the pedestal as it comes together.

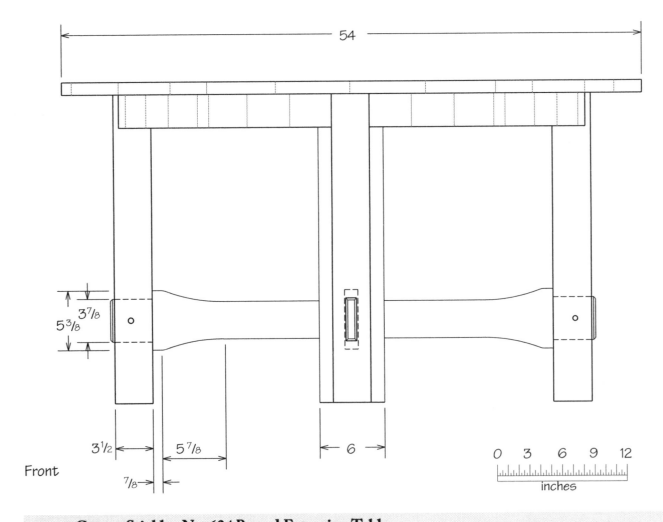

Front

Gustav Stickley No. 634 Round Extension Table

QTY	PART	SIZE	NOTES
1	Top	$1^1/8$ x 54 diameter	
16	Leg Sides	$1^1/4$ x $3^1/2$ x $27^7/8$	
4	Middle Leg Sides	$1^1/4$ x 6 x $24^7/8$	if building as extension table, double-check height required for slide mechanism
2	Middle Leg Brace	$24^7/8$ x $3/4$ x $4^{15}/16$	
1	Plate for Slides	$3/4$ x 20 x 20	plywood—adjust size to fit slide mechanism
4	Stretchers	$1^1/4$ x $5^3/8$ x $20^{15}/16$	$15^{11}/16$ between tenons—tenon extends $3/8$ beyond leg
4	Curved Aprons	$1^1/4$ x 3 x 36	rough length for bending—inside radius = $20^1/2$ finished arc length = $30^{21}/32$ between tenon shoulders

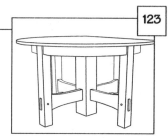

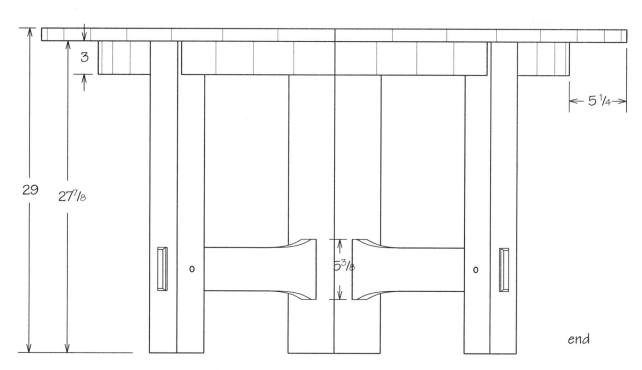

3

5 1/4

29

27 7/8

5 3/8

end

1 1/8

3

0 3 6 9 12
inches

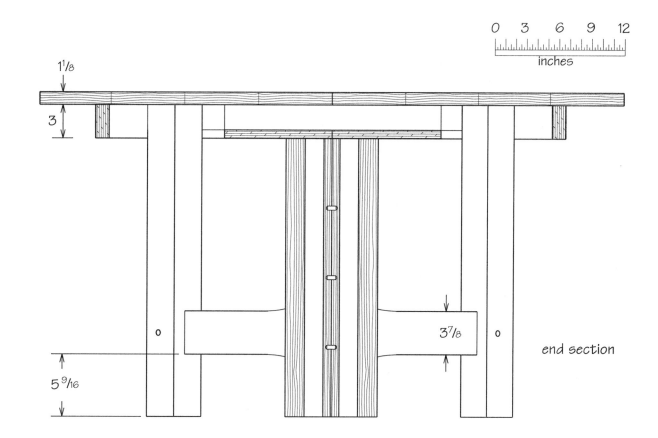

3 7/8

end section

5 9/16

plan section through legs

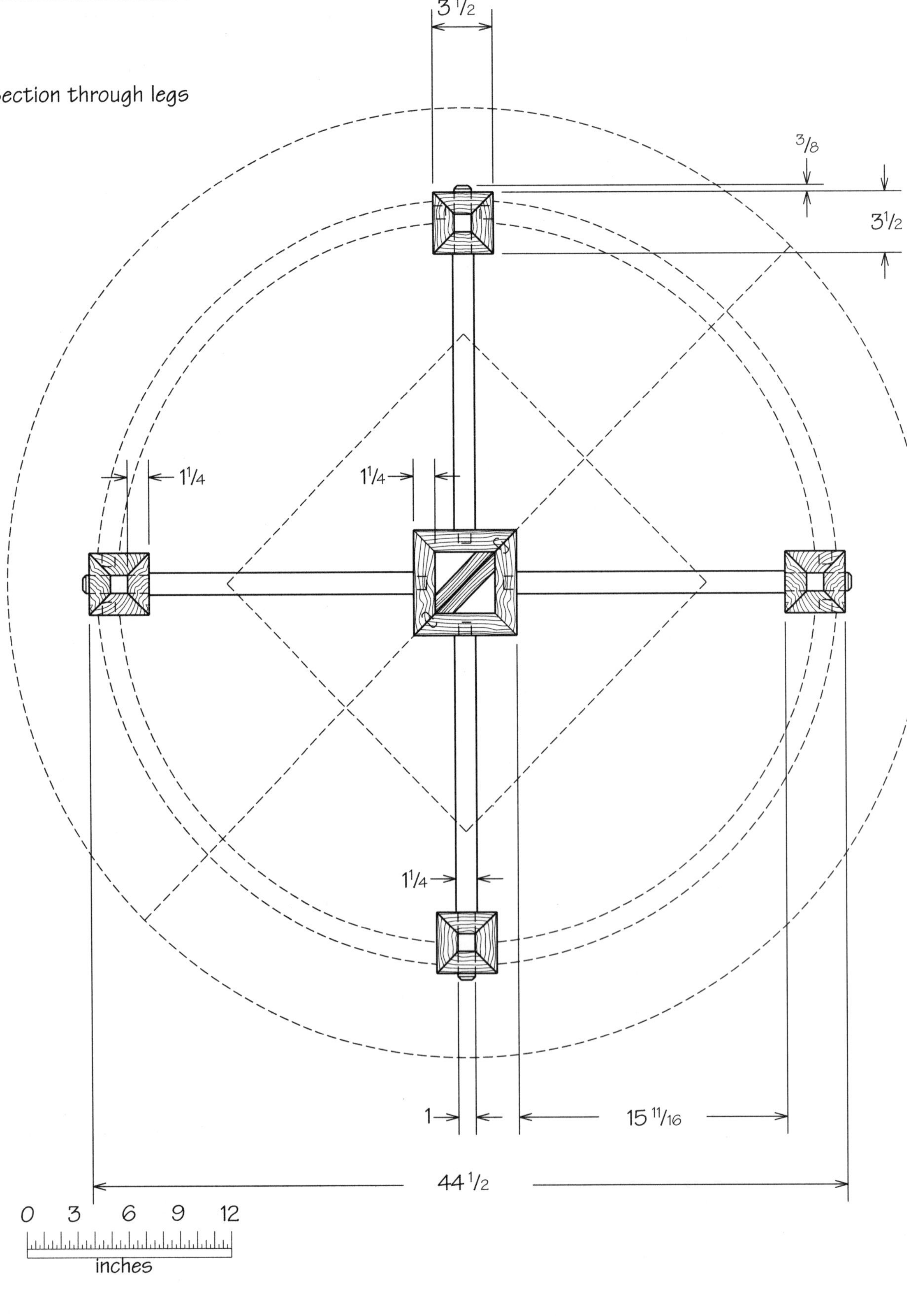

$3^{1}/_{2}$

$3/_{8}$

$3^{1}/_{2}$

$1^{1}/_{4}$

$1^{1}/_{4}$

$1^{1}/_{4}$

$1^{1}/_{4}$

1

$15^{11}/_{16}$

$44^{1}/_{2}$

0   3   6   9   12

inches

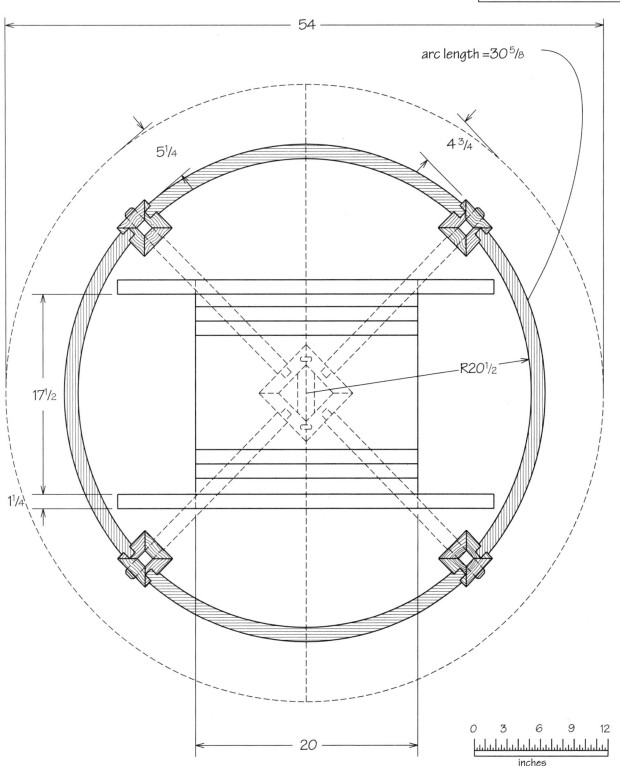

54

arc length =30 5/8

5 1/4

4 3/4

R20 1/2

17 1/2

1 1/4

20

0 3 6 9 12

inches

plan section through apron

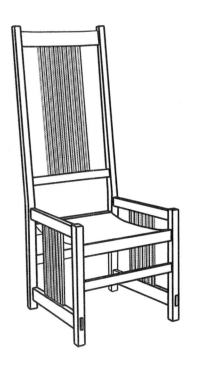

Gustav Stickley

No. 384 Side Chair

The seat cushions rest on a canvas or leather sling attached to the front and back rails with a narrow wooden cleat. Not much wood, but lots of mortises. Make full-size templates of the legs to be sure of the locations of the rails and stretchers.

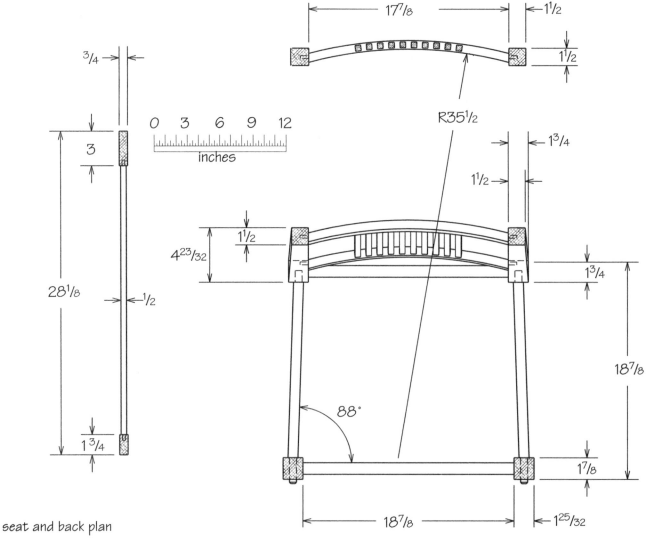

seat and back plan

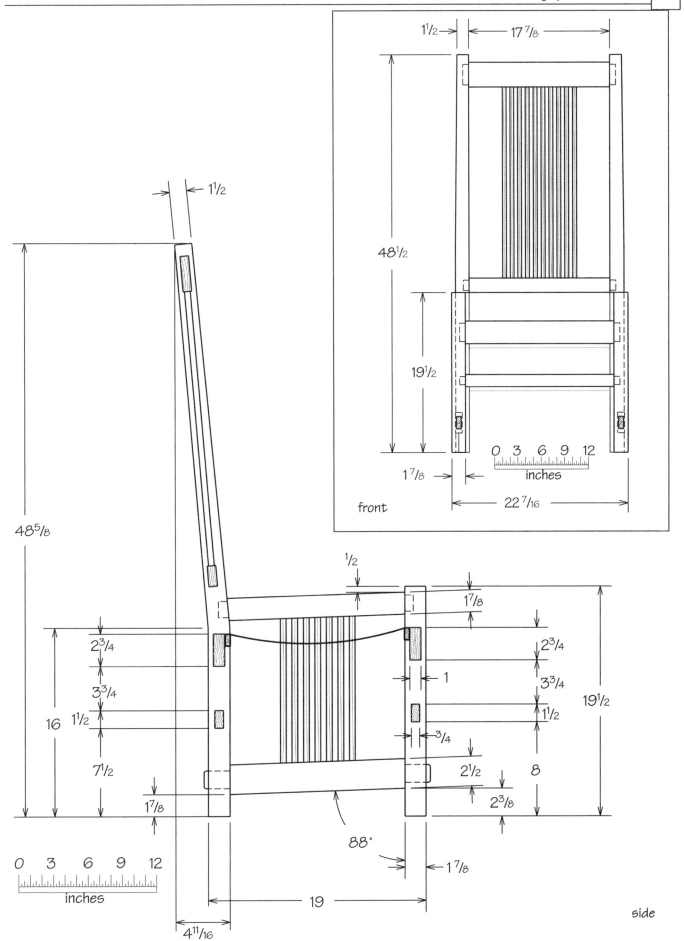

front

side

0 3 6 9 12
inches

0 3 6 9 12
inches

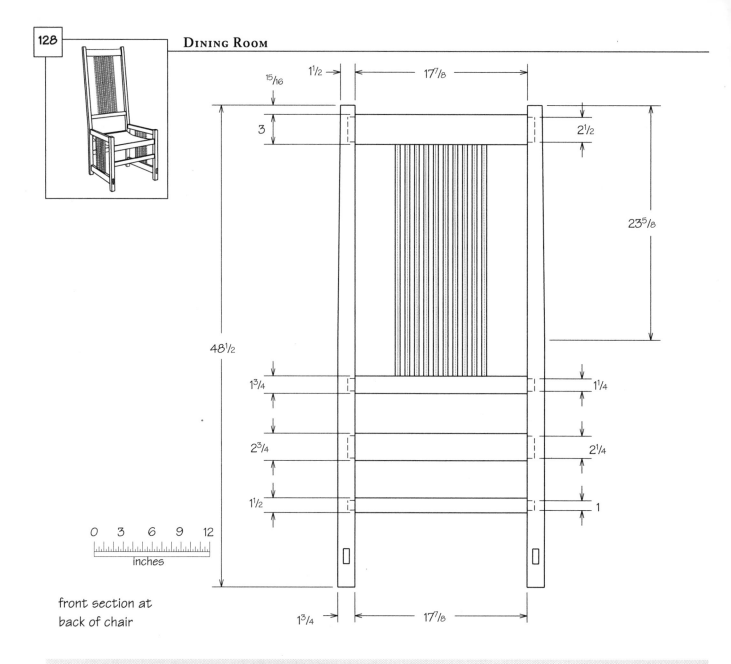

front section at
back of chair

| 0 | 3 | 6 | 9 | 12 |
inches

Gustav Stickley No. 384 Side Chair

QTY	PART	SIZE	NOTES
2	Front Legs	$1^7/_8$ x $1^7/_8$ x $19^1/_2$	
2	Back Legs	$1^3/_4$ x $4^{11}/_{16}$ x $48^5/_8$	do full size layout
1	Back Bottom Stretcher	$3/_4$ x $1^1/_2$ x $19^3/_8$	$17^7/_8$ between tenons
1	Back Stretcher @ Seat	1 x $2^1/_2$ x $19^3/_8$	$17^7/_8$ between tenons
1	Curved Back Top Stretcher	$3/_4$ x 3 x $20^1/_2$*	make long for bending—$35^1/_2$ inside radius, $17^7/_8$ between tenons
1	Curved Back Bot Stretcher	$3/_4$ x $1^3/_4$ x $20^1/_2$*	
10	Back Spindles	$1/_2$ x $1/_2$ x $24^3/_8$	$23^3/_8$ between tenons
1	Front Bottom Stretcher	$3/_4$ x $1^1/_2$ x $20^3/_8$	$18^7/_8$ between tenons
1	Front Stretcher @ Seat	1 x $2^3/_4$ x $20^3/_8$	$18^7/_8$ between tenons
2	Lower Side Stretchers	$7/_8$ x $2^1/_2$ x $20^1/_2$*	$15^1/_4$ between angled tenons—do full-size layout to determine exact size and angle
2	Upper Side Stretchers	$7/_8$ x $1^7/_8$ x $17^3/_4$	$15^5/_8$ between angled tenons—do full-size layout
14	Side Spindles	$1/_2$ x $1/_2$ x $13^1/_4$	$12^1/_4$ between angled tenons—do full-size layout
2	Canvas Cleats	$1/_2$ x 1 x 17	

Gustav Stickley

No. 386 Arm Chair

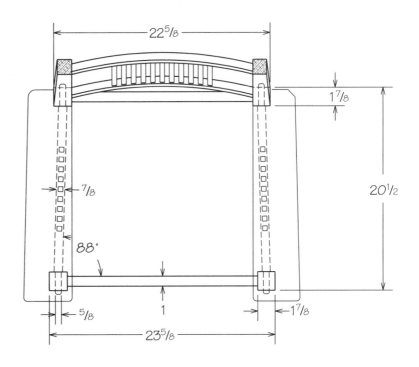

22⁵/₈

1⁷/₈

20¹/₂

⁷/₈

88°

1

5/₈

1⁷/₈

23⁵/₈

18⁷/₈   1¹/₂

1¹/₂

R35¹/₂

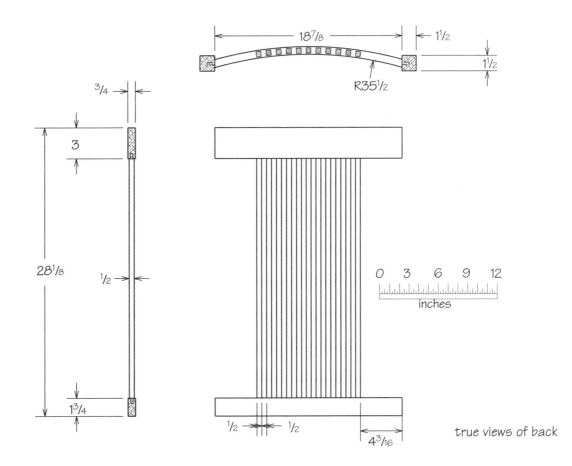

³/₄

3

28¹/₈   ¹/₂

1³/₄

0 3 6 9 12

inches

¹/₂   ¹/₂

4³/₁₆

true views of back

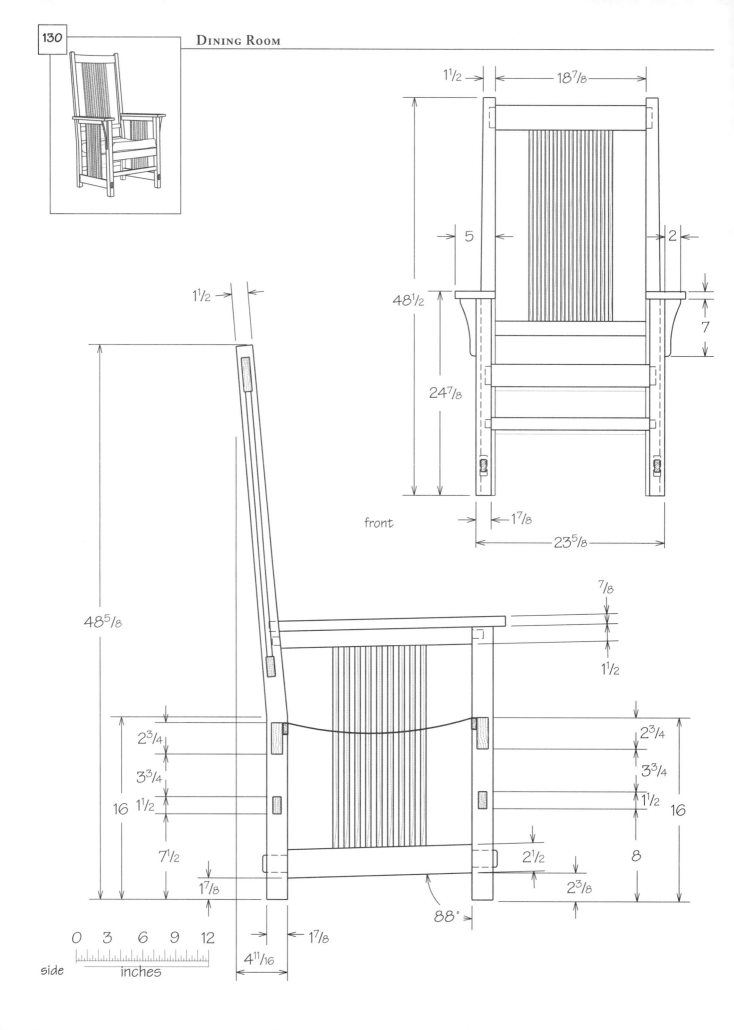

front

side

0   3   6   9   12

inches

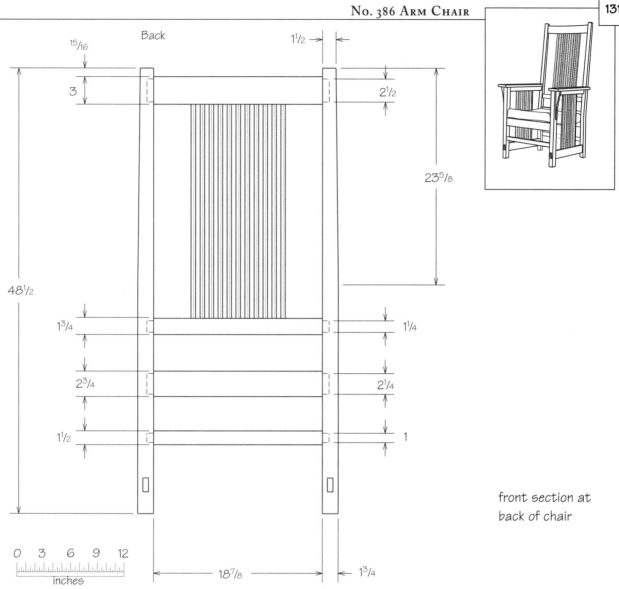

Back

$^{15}/_{16}$

3

$48^{1}/_{2}$

$1^{3}/_{4}$

$2^{3}/_{4}$

$1^{1}/_{2}$

$1^{1}/_{2}$

$2^{1}/_{2}$

$23^{5}/_{8}$

$1^{1}/_{4}$

$2^{1}/_{4}$

1

0 3 6 9 12

inches

$18^{7}/_{8}$

$1^{3}/_{4}$

front section at
back of chair

Gustav Stickley No. 386 Arm Chair

Qty	Part	Size	Notes
2	Front Legs	$1^{7}/_{8}$ x $1^{7}/_{8}$ x 24	
2	Back Legs	$1^{3}/_{4}$ x $4^{11}/_{16}$ x $48^{5}/_{8}$	do full-size layout
1	Back Bottom Stretcher	$^{3}/_{4}$ x $1^{1}/_{2}$ x $20^{3}/_{8}$	$18^{7}/_{8}$ between tenons
1	Back Stretcher @ Seat	1 x $2^{3}/_{4}$ x $20^{3}/_{8}$	$18^{7}/_{8}$ between tenons
1	Curved Back Top Stretcher	$^{3}/_{4}$ x 3 x 22*	make long for bending— $35^{1}/_{2}$ inside radius, $18^{7}/_{8}$ between tenons
1	Curved Back Bot. Stretcher	$^{3}/_{4}$ x $1^{3}/_{4}$ x 22*	
11	Back Spindles	$^{1}/_{2}$ x $^{1}/_{2}$ x $24^{3}/_{8}$	$23^{3}/_{8}$ between tenons
1	Front Bottom Stretcher	$^{3}/_{4}$ x $1^{1}/_{2}$ x $21^{7}/_{8}$	$19^{7}/_{8}$ between tenons
1	Front Stretcher @ Seat	1 x $2^{3}/_{4}$ x $21^{7}/_{8}$	$19^{7}/_{8}$ between tenons
2	Lower Side Stretchers	$^{7}/_{8}$ x $2^{1}/_{2}$ x $21^{1}/_{2}$*	$16^{3}/_{4}$ between angled tenons—do full-size layout to determine exact size and angle
2	Upper Side Stretchers	$^{7}/_{8}$ x $1^{1}/_{2}$ x $19^{1}/_{2}$	$17^{5}/_{8}$ between angled tenons—do full-size layout
18	Side Spindles	$^{1}/_{2}$ x $^{1}/_{2}$ x $18^{9}/_{16}$	$17^{9}/_{16}$ between angled tenons—do full-size layout
2	Arms	$^{7}/_{8}$ x 5 x $22^{1}/_{2}$	notch corner @ back leg
2	Canvas Cleats	$^{1}/_{2}$ x 1 x $18^{1}/_{2}$	

Gustav Stickley

NO. 802 SIDEBOARD
36" high x 42" wide x 18" deep

This is one of the few pieces that has a rail above the drawers. The back rail under the top has no arch.

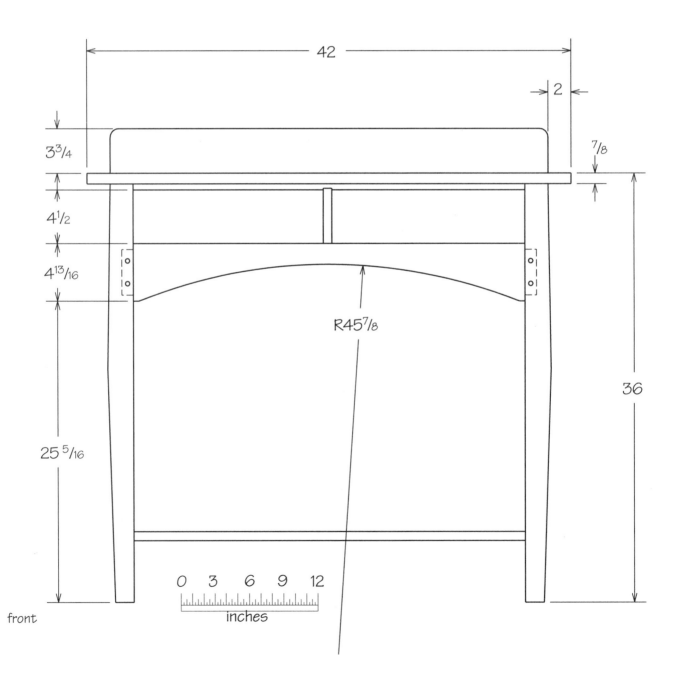

42

2

3³/4

⁷/8

4¹/2

4¹³/16

R45⁷/8

36

25 ⁵/16

0   3   6   9   12
inches

front

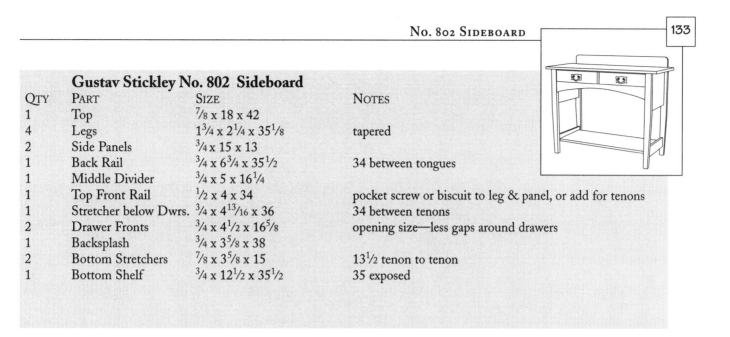

Gustav Stickley No. 802 Sideboard

QTY	PART	SIZE	NOTES
1	Top	$^7/_8$ x 18 x 42	
4	Legs	$1^3/_4$ x $2^1/_4$ x $35^1/_8$	tapered
2	Side Panels	$^3/_4$ x 15 x 13	
1	Back Rail	$^3/_4$ x $6^3/_4$ x $35^1/_2$	34 between tongues
1	Middle Divider	$^3/_4$ x 5 x $16^1/_4$	
1	Top Front Rail	$^1/_2$ x 4 x 34	pocket screw or biscuit to leg & panel, or add for tenons
1	Stretcher below Dwrs.	$^3/_4$ x $4^{13}/_{16}$ x 36	34 between tenons
2	Drawer Fronts	$^3/_4$ x $4^1/_2$ x $16^5/_8$	opening size—less gaps around drawers
1	Backsplash	$^3/_4$ x $3^5/_8$ x 38	
2	Bottom Stretchers	$^7/_8$ x $3^5/_8$ x 15	$13^1/_2$ tenon to tenon
1	Bottom Shelf	$^3/_4$ x $12^1/_2$ x $35^1/_2$	35 exposed

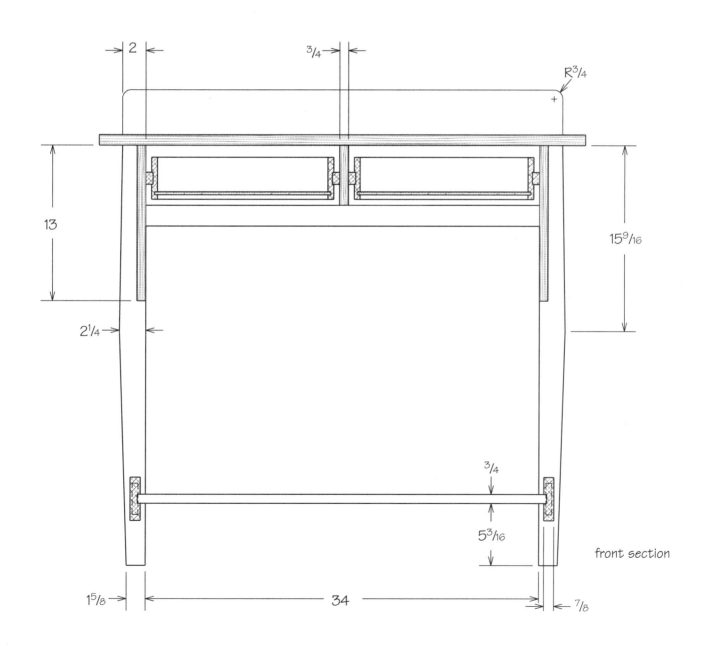

front section

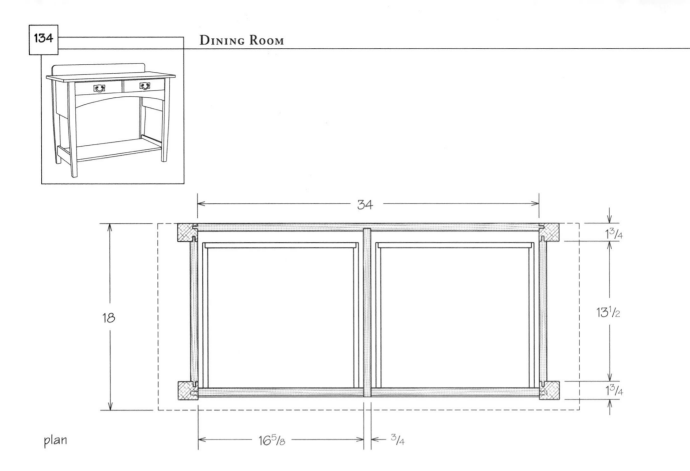

plan

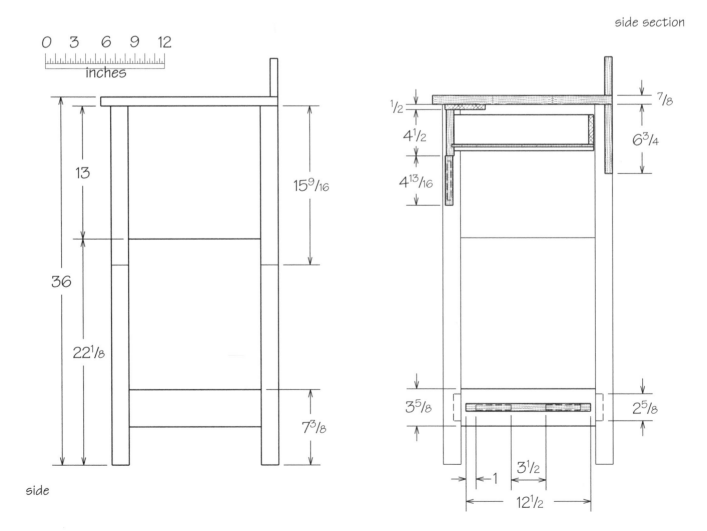

0 3 6 9 12
inches

side

side section

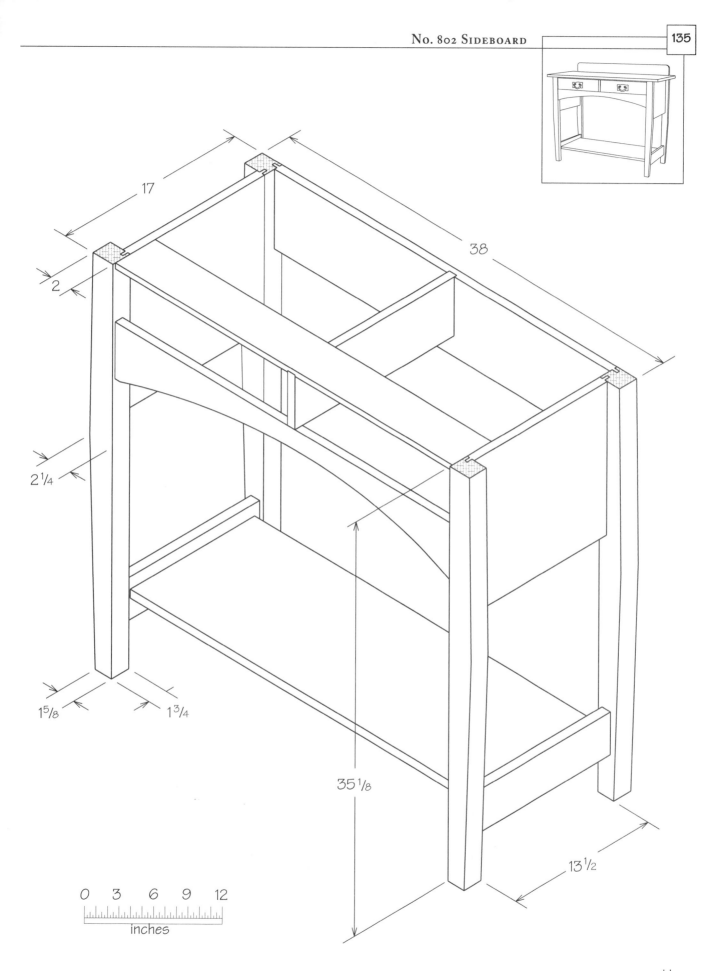

17

2

38

2¹/₄

1⁵/₈   1³/₄

35¹/₈

13¹/₂

0   3   6   9   12
inches

assembly

Gustav Stickley

NO. 815 CHINA CABINET

42" wide x 15" deep x 66" high

The catalog describes this china cabinet as having "fixed shelves along the lines of the mullions." Don't attach the shelves until finishing is complete and the glass is in place. The shelves can be permanently attached by screwing through cleats recessed below, or by pegs in holes drilled in the stiles.

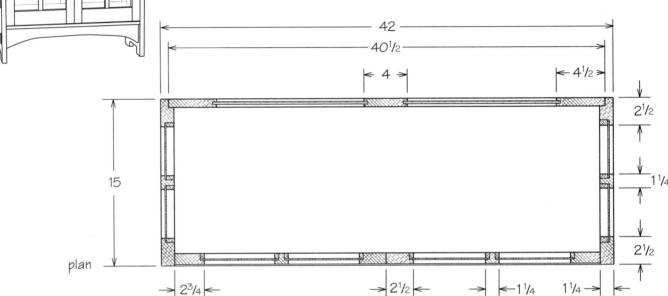

plan

Gustav Stickley No. 815 China Cabinet

QTY	PART	SIZE	NOTES
2	Sides	$1\frac{1}{4}$ x 15 x 65	parts detailed below
4	Side Stiles	$1\frac{1}{4}$ x $2\frac{1}{2}$ x 65	
2	Side Top Rails	$1\frac{1}{4}$ x $5\frac{3}{4}$ x 12	10 between tenon shoulders
2	Side Bottom Rails	$1\frac{1}{4}$ x 14 x 12	10 between tenon shoulders
2	Side Mullions	$1\frac{1}{4}$ x $1\frac{1}{4}$ x $47\frac{3}{4}$	$46\frac{1}{4}$ between tenon shoulders
12	Side Muntins	$1\frac{1}{4}$ x $1\frac{1}{4}$ x $4\frac{7}{8}$	$4\frac{3}{8}$ between tenon shoulders
1	Top	1 x 15 x $42\frac{3}{4}$	$39\frac{1}{2}$ between tenon shoulders
1	Bottom	$\frac{13}{16}$ x 15 x $40\frac{1}{2}$	$39\frac{1}{2}$ between tenon shoulders
2	Front & Back Aprons	$1\frac{1}{4}$ x $5\frac{3}{8}$ x $42\frac{3}{4}$	$39\frac{1}{2}$ between tenon shoulders
1	Backsplash	1 x 3 x $39\frac{1}{2}$	
1	Paneled Back	$\frac{3}{4}$ x $40\frac{1}{2}$ x $53\frac{1}{8}$	$39\frac{1}{2}$ x $52\frac{1}{8}$ opening between rabbets—parts detailed below
2	Outer Back Stiles	$\frac{3}{4}$ x $4\frac{1}{2}$ x $53\frac{1}{8}$	4 x $52\frac{1}{8}$ exposed
2	Back-Top & Bot. Rails	$\frac{3}{4}$ x $4\frac{1}{2}$ x $32\frac{1}{2}$	4 exposed width—$31\frac{1}{2}$ between tenon shoulders
1	Back- Middle Stile	$\frac{3}{4}$ x 4 x $45\frac{1}{8}$	$44\frac{1}{8}$ between tenon shoulders
2	Back-Middle Rails	$\frac{3}{4}$ x 4 x $14\frac{3}{4}$	$13\frac{3}{4}$ between tenon shoulders
4	Back Panels	$\frac{1}{4}$ x $14\frac{3}{4}$ x $21\frac{1}{16}$	$13\frac{3}{4}$ x 20 1/16 exposed
2	Doors	1 x $19\frac{3}{4}$ x $52\frac{1}{8}$	opening size—trim for desired gaps—parts detailed below
2	Door Hinge Stiles	1 x $2\frac{3}{4}$ x $52\frac{1}{8}$	
2	Door Inner Stiles	1 x $2\frac{1}{2}$ x $52\frac{1}{8}$	
2	Door Top Rails	1 x $2\frac{3}{4}$ x $15\frac{1}{2}$	$14\frac{1}{2}$ between tenon shoulders
2	Door Bottom Rails	1 x $4\frac{1}{8}$ x $15\frac{1}{2}$	$14\frac{1}{2}$ between tenon shoulders
2	Door Mullions	1 x $1\frac{1}{4}$ x $46\frac{1}{4}$	$45\frac{1}{4}$ between tenon shoulders
12	Door Muntins	1 x $1\frac{1}{4}$ x $7\frac{1}{2}$	$6\frac{5}{8}$ between tenon shoulders
3	Shelves	$\frac{3}{4}$ x $13\frac{1}{8}$ x $39\frac{1}{2}$	opening size—make smaller for adjustable shelves

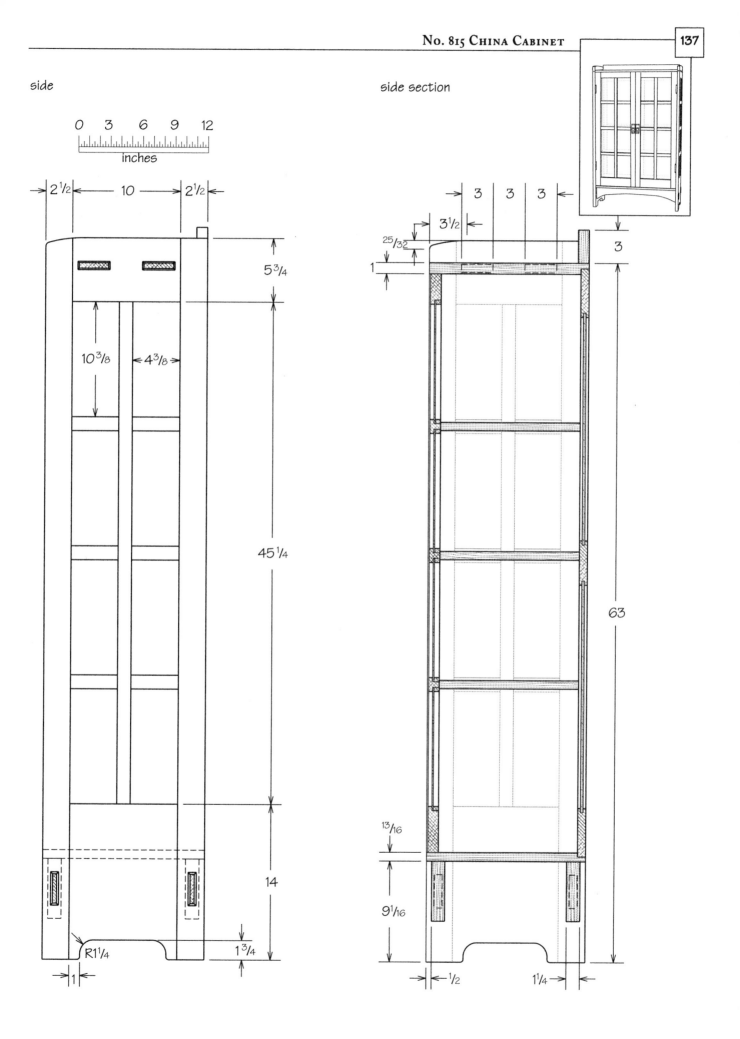

side

side section

0 3 6 9 12
inches

2½   10   2½

5¾

10⅜   ←4⅜→

45¼

14

R1¼   1¾

1

3   3   3

3½

25/32

1

3

63

13/16

9 1/16

½   1¼

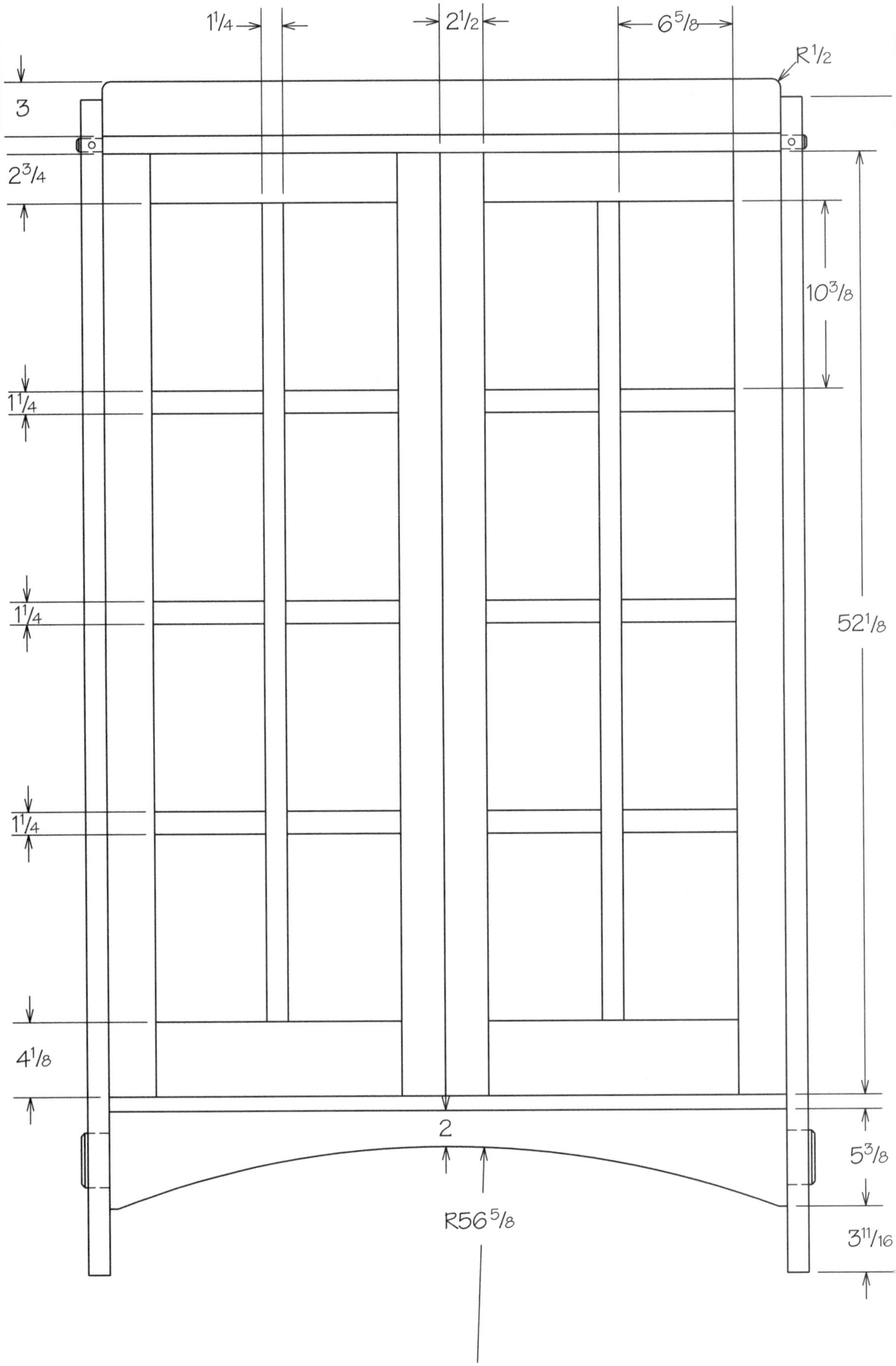

$1\frac{1}{4}$

$2\frac{1}{2}$

$6\frac{5}{8}$

$R\frac{1}{2}$

3

$2\frac{3}{4}$

$10\frac{3}{8}$

$1\frac{1}{4}$

$52\frac{1}{8}$

$1\frac{1}{4}$

$1\frac{1}{4}$

$4\frac{1}{8}$

2

$5\frac{3}{8}$

$R56\frac{5}{8}$

$3\frac{11}{16}$

front

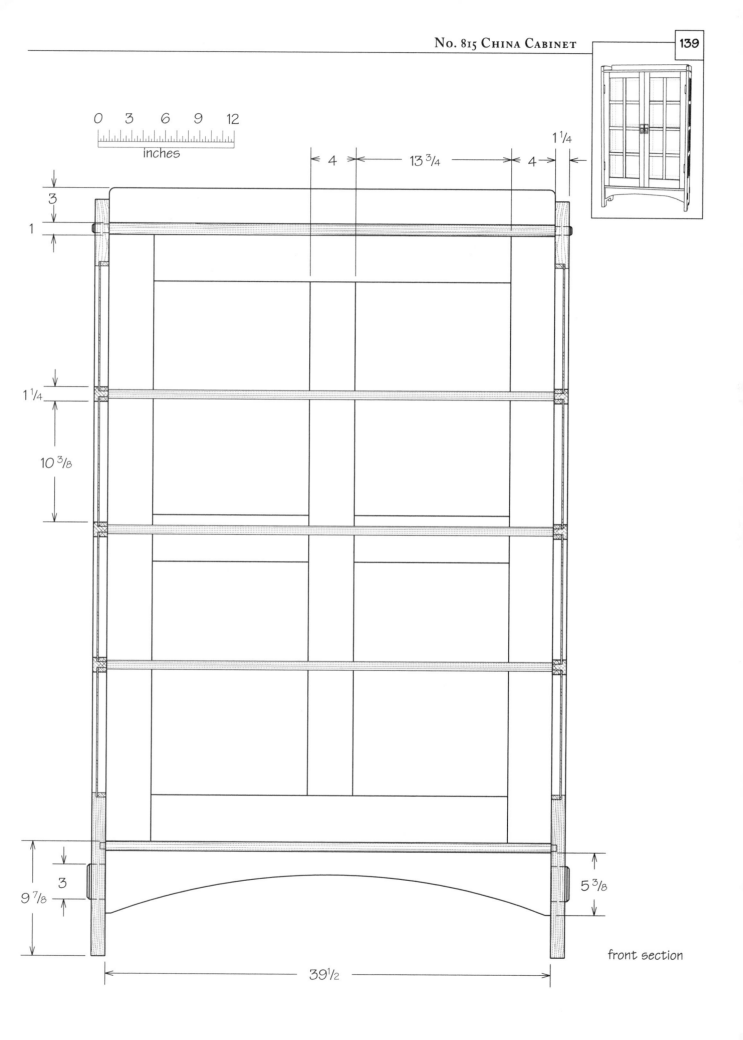

0   3   6   9   12
inches

4   13³/₄   4   1¹/₄

3
1

1¹/₄

10³/₈

9⁷/₈   3

5³/₈

39¹/₂

front section

Gustav Stickley

NO. 814 SIDEBOARD

45" high x 60" long x 22" deep

A modestly sized sideboard with room for storing table linens, silverware, or anything else that doesn't need to be on display. An investment in reproduction hardware would be well worth it, although this piece is also quite attractive with regular hinges and pulls.

See the chapter on construction options for alternate ways to make the legs.

Gustav Stickley No. 814 Sideboard

QTY	PART	SIZE	NOTES
1	Top	$3/4$ x 22 x 60	
4	Legs	$2^3/4$ x $2^3/4$ x $35^1/4$	
2	Top, Side Rail	$3/4$ x $2^3/8$ x $20^1/2$	$15^1/2$ between tenon shoulders
2	Bot., Side Rail	$3/4$ x $3^1/4$ x $20^1/2$	$15^1/2$ between tenon shoulders
2	Side Panels	$1/2$ x $16^1/4$ x $22^1/16$	$15^1/2$ x $21^5/16$ exposed
1	Bottom-Frame & Panel	$3/4$ x $19^1/2$ x $52^3/4$	parts detailed below—$19^1/4$ x 52 exposed—notch @ legs
1	Bot. Back Rail	$3/4$ x $4^1/4$ x $47^1/2$	$46^3/4$ between tenon shoulders
1	Bot. Front Rail	$3/4$ x $3^1/4$ x $47^1/2$	$46^3/4$ between tenon shoulders
2	Bot. End Stile	$3/4$ x 3 x $19^1/4$	
1	Bot. Mid Stile	$3/4$ x 3 x $12^1/2$	$11^3/4$ between tenon shoulders
2	Bot. Panels	$1/4$ x $12^1/2$ x $22^5/8$	$11^3/4$ x $21^7/8$ exposed
1	Back-frame & Panel	$3/4$ x $24^1/2$ x $50^3/4$	parts detailed below—$24^1/2$ x 50 exposed
2	Outer Stiles	$3/4$ x $4^3/8$ x $24^1/2$	4 exposed
2	Inner Stiles	$3/4$ x 4 x $9^5/8$	$8^7/8$ between tenon shoulders
3	Top, Mid, & Bot. Rail	$3/4$ x 4 x $42^3/4$	42 between tenon shoulders
3	Upper Back Panels	$1/4$ x $9^5/8$ x $12^1/16$	$8^7/8$ x $11^5/16$ exposed
1	Lower Back Panel	$1/4$ x $4^3/8$ x $42^3/4$	$3^5/8$ x 42 exposed
1	Shelf	$3/4$ x $19^3/8$ x $52^3/4$	plywood—$19^1/8$ x 52 exposed—notch @ legs
1	Shelf Edge	$3/4$ x $1^1/8$ x 50	$1/4$ x $3/8$ tongue into groove in plywood
2	Divider Panels	$3/4$ x $20^1/2$ x $15^5/8$	parts detailed below—$20^1/4$ x $15^3/8$ exposed—notch for top rail
4	Stiles	$3/4$ x 3 x $15^5/8$	
4	Rails	$3/4$ x 3 x $15^1/4$	$14^1/2$ between tenon shoulders
2	Panels	$1/4$ x $15^1/4$ x $10^3/8$	$9^5/8$ x $14^1/2$ exposed
1	Front Apron	$3/4$ x $2^3/4$ x 53	50 between tenon shoulders
1	Front Top Rail	$3/4$ x $2^1/2$ x 50	biscuit or pocket screw to legs, or add tenons
1	Back Top Rail	$3/4$ x 2 x 50	biscuit or pocket screw to legs, or add tenons
2	Hinge Strips	$3/8$ x $2^1/2$ x $14^5/8$	
2	Doors	$3/4$ x $15^3/4$ x $14^5/8$	opening size—trim for desired gaps
1	Drawer Front	$3/4$ x $4^7/8$ x $16^1/4$	opening size—trim for desired gaps
1	Drawer Front	$3/4$ x $4^3/8$ x $16^1/4$	opening size—trim for desired gaps
1	Drawer Front	$3/4$ x $3^7/8$ x $16^1/4$	opening size—trim for desired gaps
1	Drawer Front	$3/4$ x $5^5/8$ x 50	opening size—trim for desired gaps
2	Plate Rack Uprights	$3/4$ x $2^1/8$ x $8^7/8$	taper to $1^1/2$
1	Plate Rack Top Rail	$1/2$ x $2^3/4$ x $54^1/4$	taper to 2 @ ends, trim flush to outer edge of uprights
2	Plate Rack Mid, Bot. Rail	$1/2$ x $1^3/4$ x $54^1/4$	trim flush to outer edge of uprights

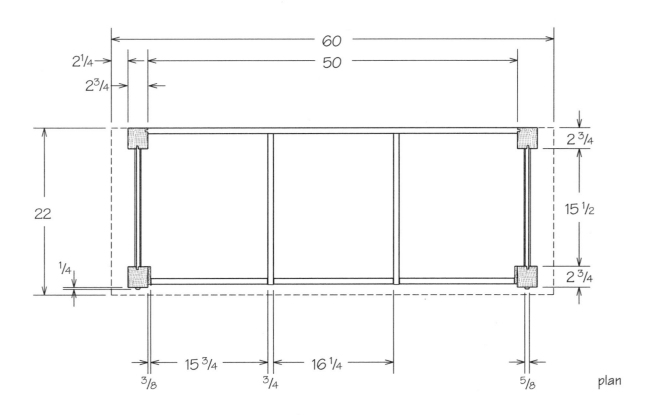

plan

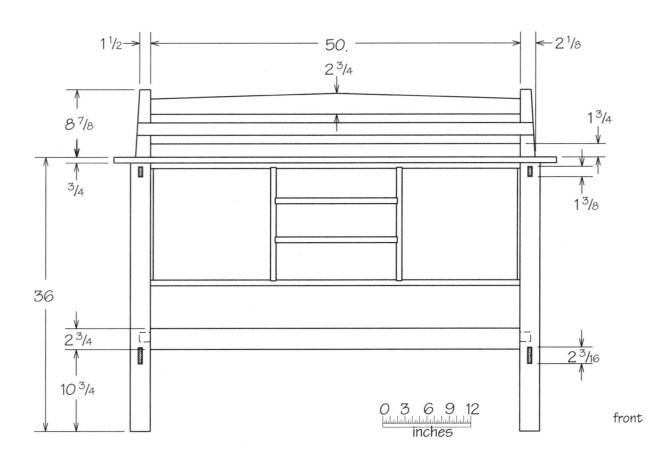

0 3 6 9 12
inches

front

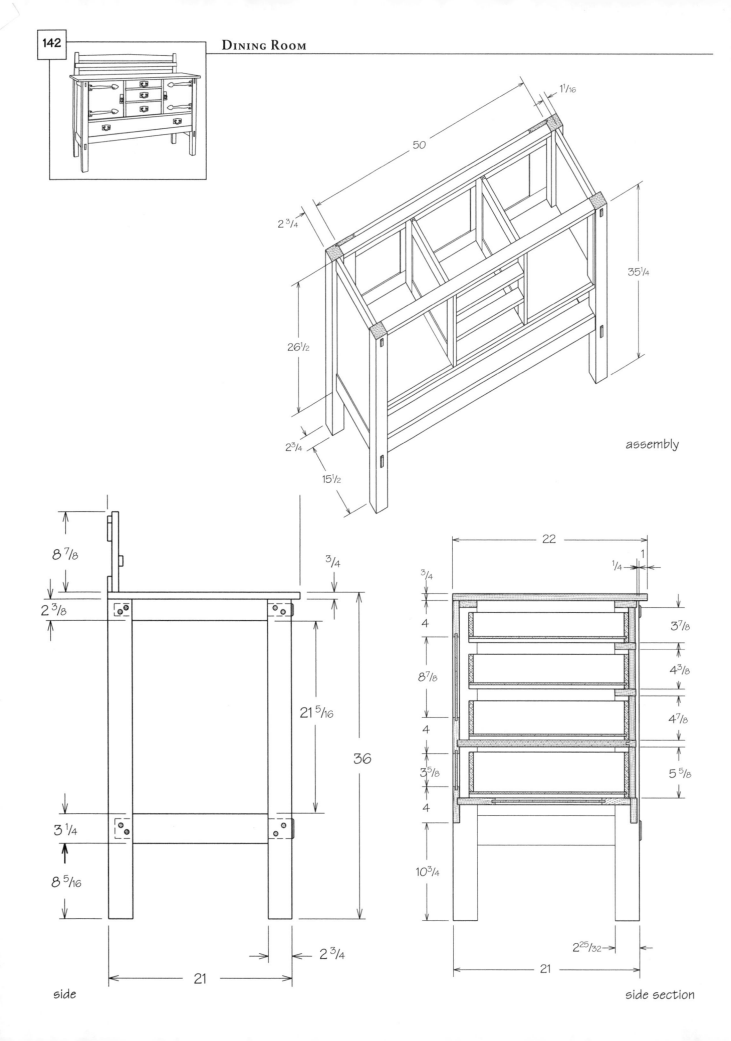

2³/₄

1¹/₁₆

50

35¹/₄

26¹/₂

2³/₄

15¹/₂

assembly

8⁷/₈

³/₄

2³/₈

21⁵/₁₆

36

3¹/₄

8⁵/₁₆

2³/₄

21

side

22

1

³/₄

¹/₄

³/₄

3⁷/₈

4

8⁷/₈

4³/₈

4⁷/₈

4

3⁵/₈

5⁵/₈

4

10³/₄

2²⁵/₃₂

21

side section

INDEX

FURTHER READING

Gustav Stickley
  Making Authentic Craftsman Furniture, 1986,
  Dover Publications
  Craftsman Homes, 1979, Dover Publications

David M. Cathers
  Furniture of the American Arts And Crafts
  Movement, 1996, Turn of the Century
  Editions

Mary Ann Smith
  Gustav Stickley, the Craftsman, 1983, Dover
  Publications

Bruce Johnson
  The Official Identification and Price Guide to
  Arts and Crafts, 1988, The House of
  Collectibles

R. Bruce Hoadley
  Understanding Wood, 1982, revised 2001, The
  Taunton Press

Reproductions of Original Furniture
Manufacturer's Catalogs
  Stickley Craftsman Furniture Catalogs, 1979,
  Dover Publications (Catalog of Craftsman
  Furniture made by Gustav Stickley at the
  Craftsman Workshops, Eastwood N.Y. 1910)

The Work of L. & J.G. Stickley, Fayetteville,
N.Y. ca.1914

Collected Works of Gustav Stickley, edited by
Stephen Gray and Robert Edwards, 1981,
Turn of the Century Editions (catalog 1904,
retail plates 1907, articles and illustrations
from "The Craftsman" various dates, 1901-
1914)

Early L. & J.G. Stickley Furniture, edited by
Donald Davidoff and Robert L. Zarrow, 1992,
Dover Publications (1906-1909 Catalog, retail
plates ca. 1909)

Limbert Arts And Crafts Furniture, The
Complete 1903 Catalog, 1992 Dover
Publications

Roycroft Furniture Catalog, 1906, 1994,
Dover Publications

The 1912 And 1915 Gustav Stickley
Craftsman Furniture Catalogs, 1991, Dover
Publications

ACKNOWLEDGMENTS

Special thanks to Bud Young of The Carpenter's House in Alexandria, Ohio.

LARGE-FORMAT PRINTS

Large-format prints of the project plans in this book are also available. These prints are plotted directly from AutoCAD, with color enhancements. Each set of prints includes regular orthographic views, details and sections, plus a bill of materials. For ordering information and prices, please contact Cambium Books, 800-238-7724 or on the web at www.CAMBIUMBOOKS.com, or go to the author's website, www.CRAFTSMANPLANS.com.